MAX AXIOM AND THE SOCIETY OF SUPER SCIENTISTS

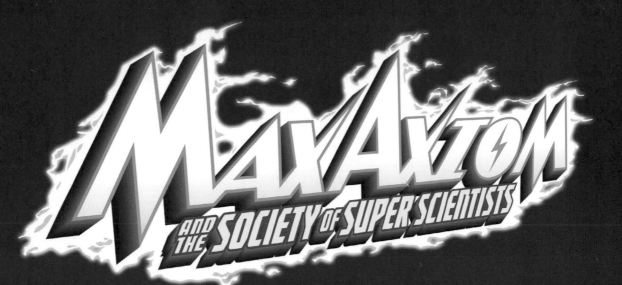

RETURNING TO THE MOON

BY BRUCE BERGLUND
ILLUSTRATED BY EDUARDO GARCIA

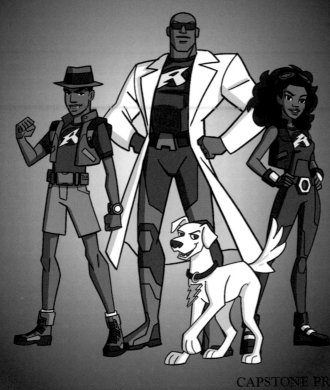

CAPSTONE PRESS
a capstone imprint

Published by Capstone Press, an imprint of Capstone.
1710 Roe Crest Drive North Mankato, Minnesota 56003
capstonepub.com

Library of Congress Cataloging-in-Publication Data
is available on the Library of Congress website.
ISBN: 9781666337242 (hardcover)
ISBN: 9781666337181 (paperback)
ISBN: 9781666337198 (ebook PDF)

Summary: On July 20, 1969, Neil Armstrong became the first person to set foot on the moon. However, no person has visited the moon since 1972. Today, NASA is planning to go back for the first time in more than 50 years. Tag along with Max Axiom and the Society of Super Scientists to learn how NASA plans to finally return and have a permanent base on the moon.

Editorial Credits
Editor: Aaron Sautter; Designer: Brann Garvey; Media Researcher: Morgan Walters; Production Specialist: Polly Fisher

All internet sites appearing in back matter were available and accurate when this book was sent to press.

Printed and bound in the USA.

TABLE OF CONTENTS

SECTION 1:
THE FIRST TRIP TO THE MOON   6

SECTION 2:
ROCKET POWER   10

SECTION 3:
TRAVELING THROUGH SPACE   16

SECTION 4:
BACK TO THE MOON   22

MOONWALKING..28
GLOSSARY..30
READ MORE...31
INTERNET SITES..31
INDEX...32
ABOUT THE AUTHOR..32

THE SOCIETY OF SUPER SCIENTISTS

MAX AXIOM

After years of study, Max Axiom, the world's first Super Scientist, knew the mysteries of the universe were too vast for one person alone to uncover. So Max created the Society of Super Scientists! Using their superpowers and super-smarts, this talented group investigates today's most urgent scientific and environmental issues and learns about actions everyone can take to solve them.

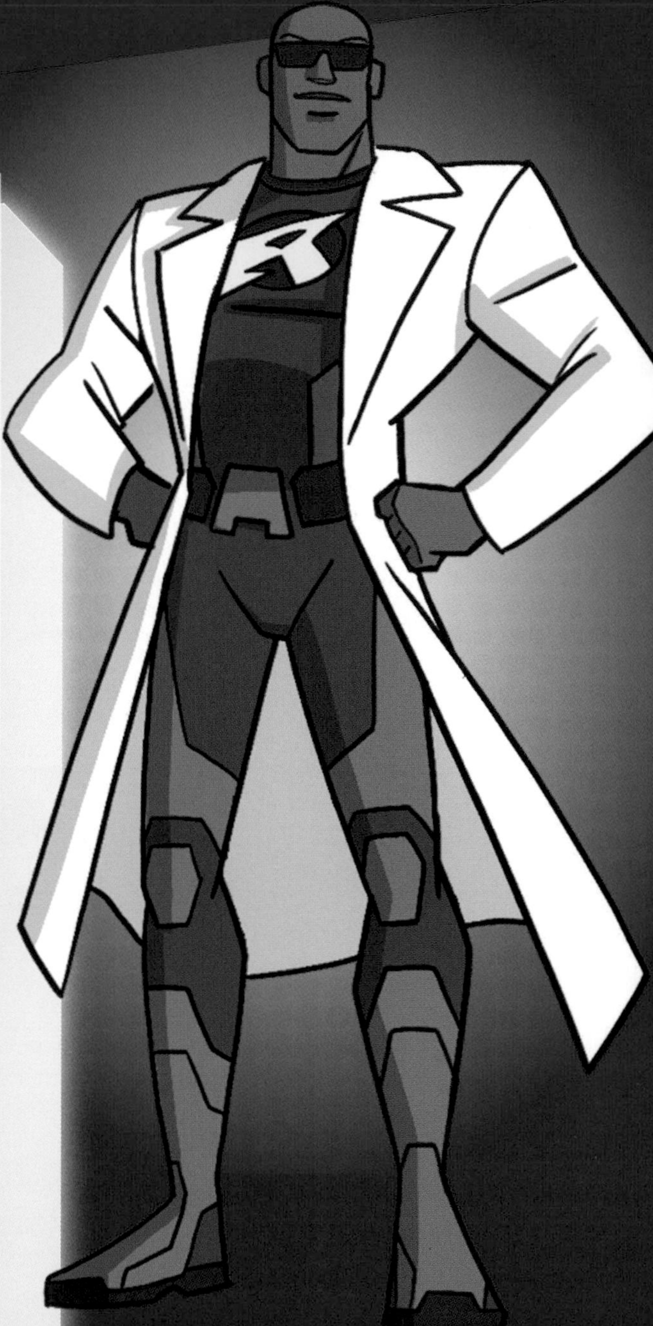

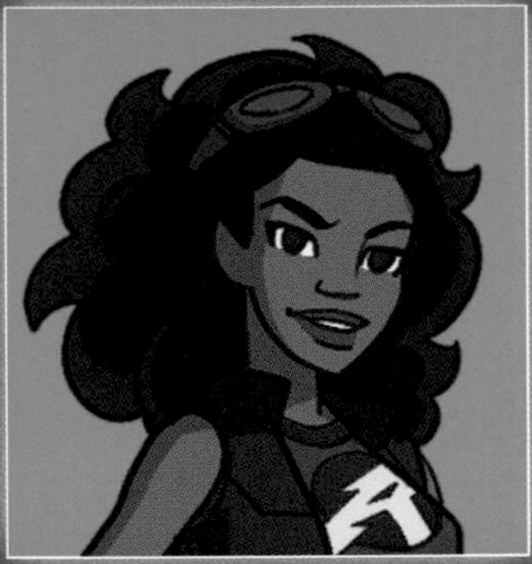

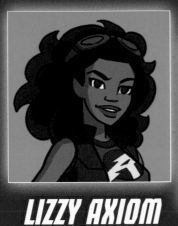

LIZZY AXIOM

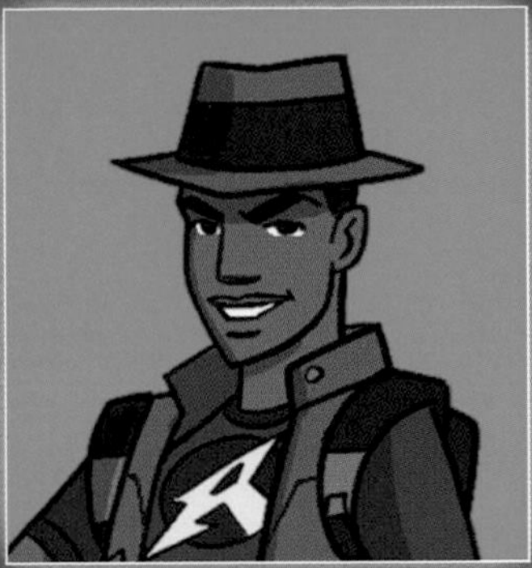

NICK AXIOM

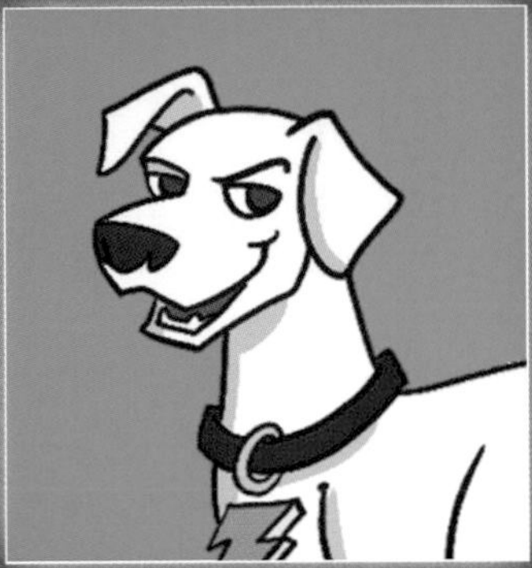

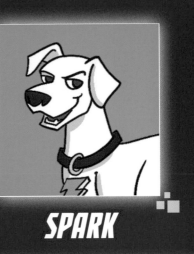

SPARK

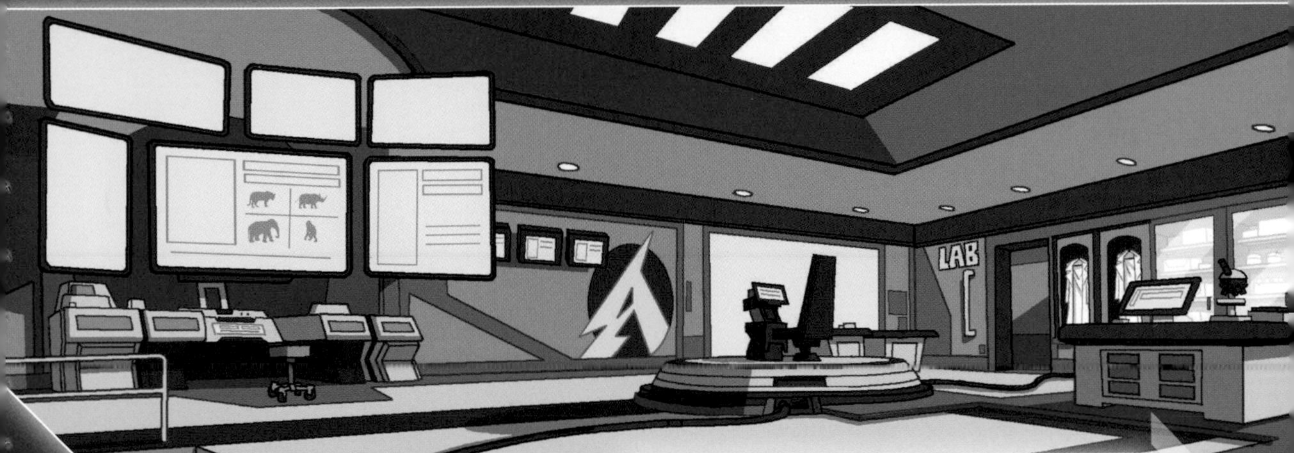
LAB

THE DISCOVERY LAB

Home of the Society of Super Scientists, this state-of-the-art lab houses advanced tools for cutting-edge research and radical scientific innovation. More importantly, it is a space for Super Scientists to collaborate and share knowledge as they work together to tackle any challenge.

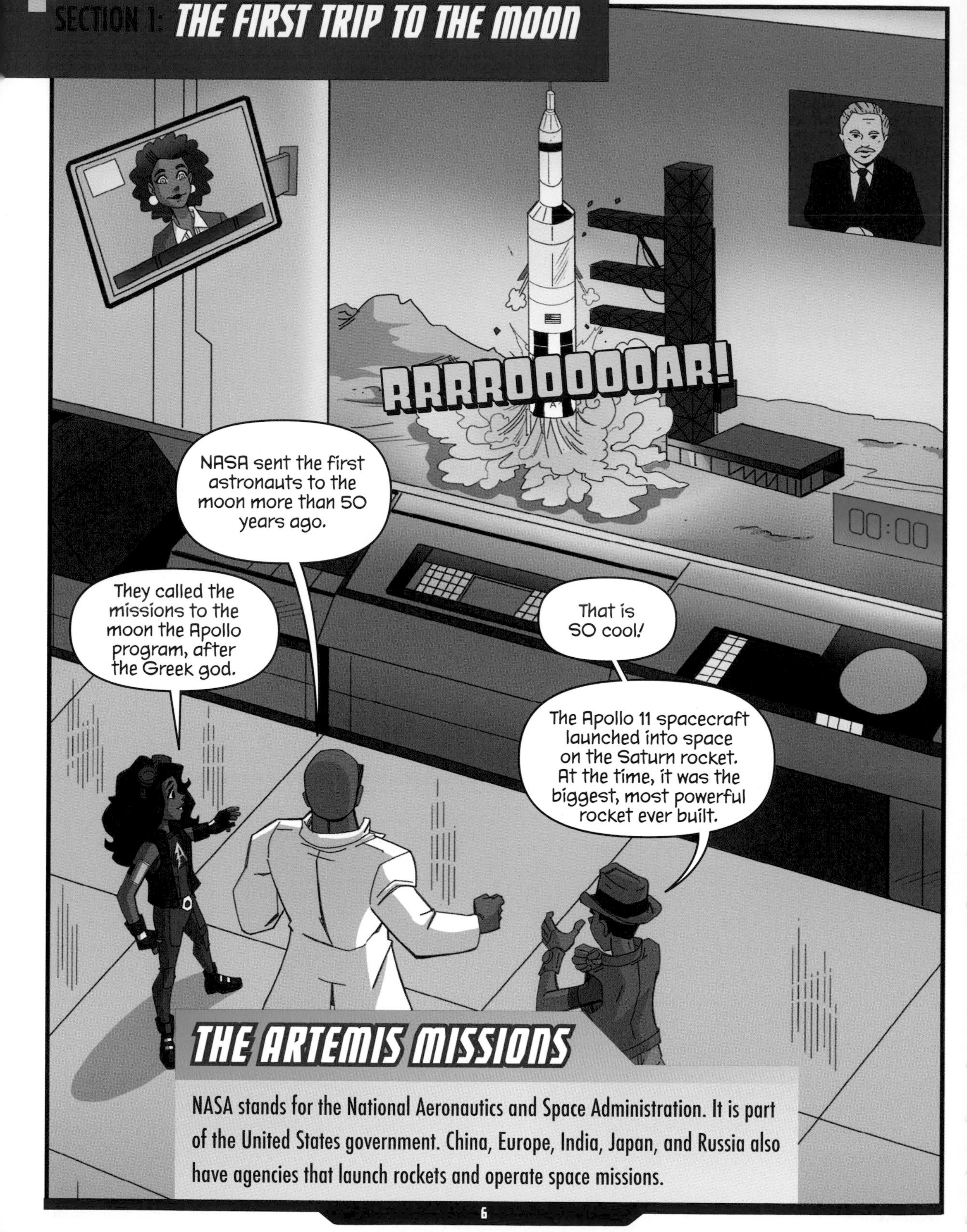
RRRROOOOOAR!
NASA sent the first astronauts to the moon more than 50 years ago.
They called the missions to the moon the Apollo program, after the Greek god.
That is SO cool!
The Apollo 11 spacecraft launched into space on the Saturn rocket. At the time, it was the biggest, most powerful rocket ever built.

THE ARTEMIS MISSIONS

NASA stands for the National Aeronautics and Space Administration. It is part of the United States government. China, Europe, India, Japan, and Russia also have agencies that launch rockets and operate space missions.

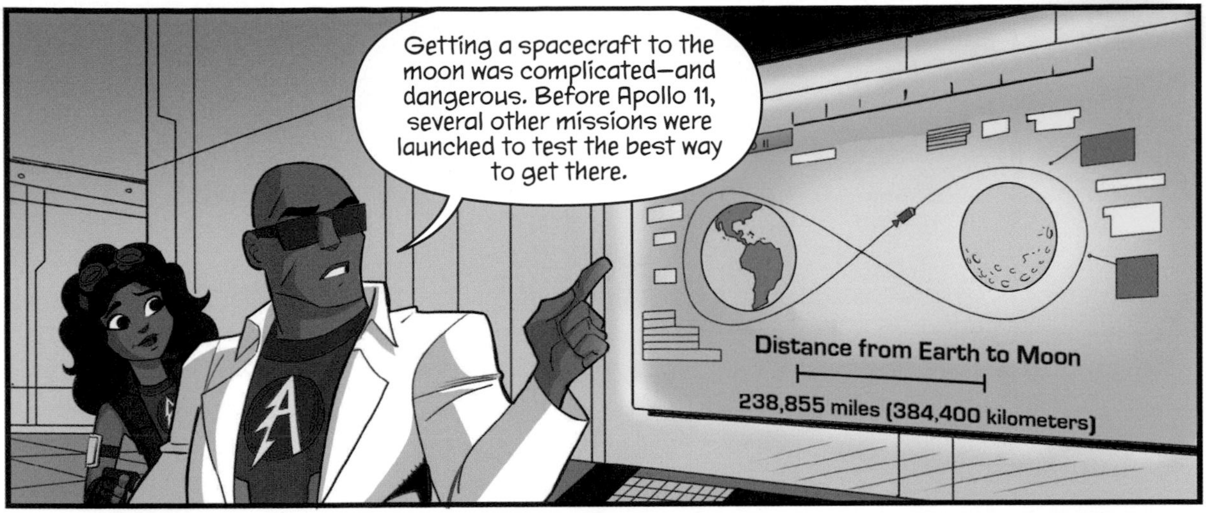
Getting a spacecraft to the moon was complicated—and dangerous. Before Apollo 11, several other missions were launched to test the best way to get there.
Distance from Earth to Moon
238,855 miles (384,400 kilometers)

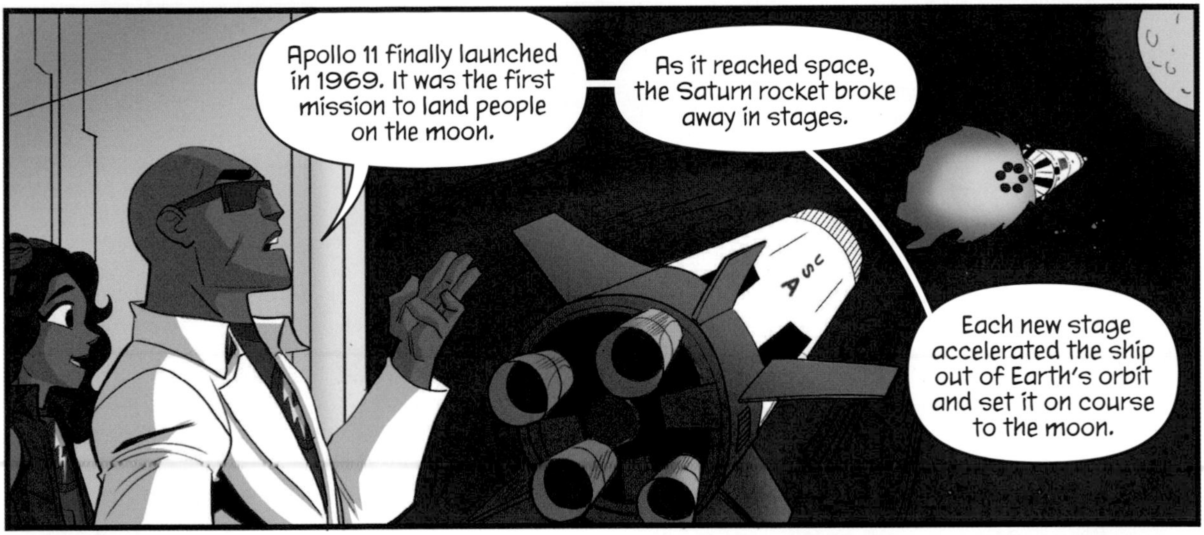
Apollo 11 finally launched in 1969. It was the first mission to land people on the moon.
As it reached space, the Saturn rocket broke away in stages.
Each new stage accelerated the ship out of Earth's orbit and set it on course to the moon.

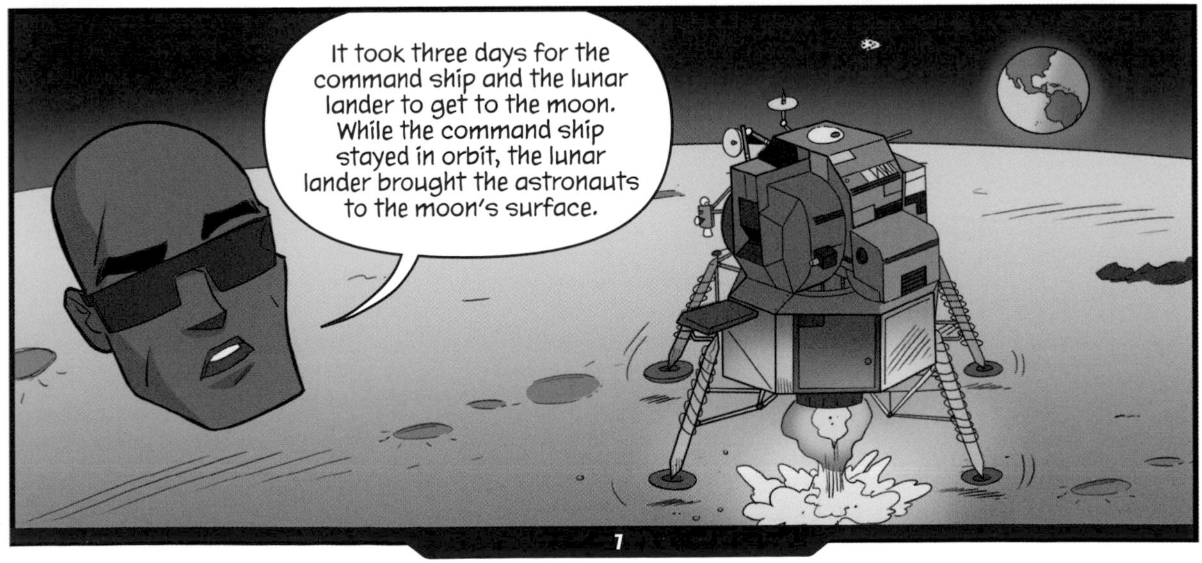
It took three days for the command ship and the lunar lander to get to the moon. While the command ship stayed in orbit, the lunar lander brought the astronauts to the moon's surface.

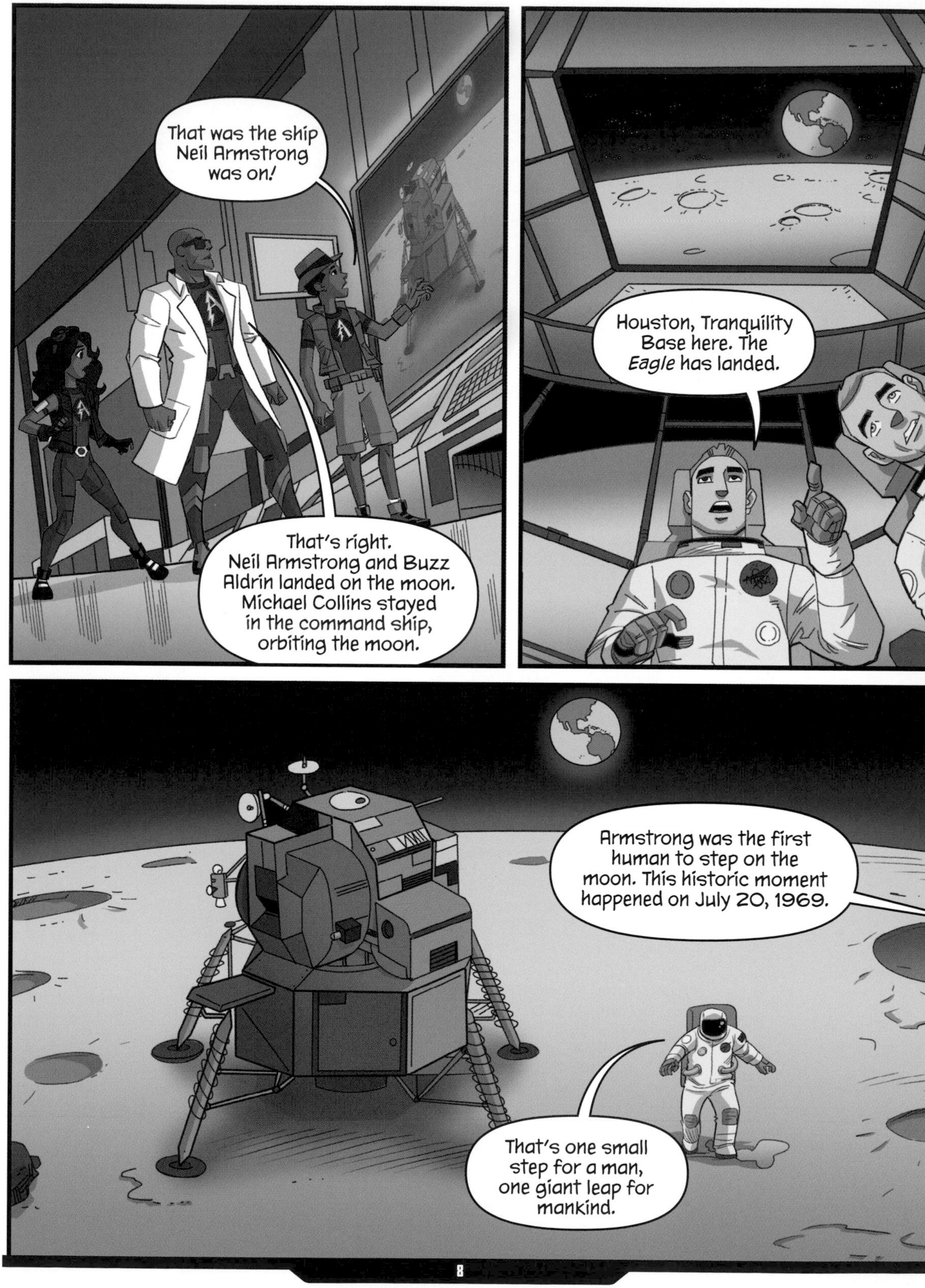
That was the ship Neil Armstrong was on!
That's right. Neil Armstrong and Buzz Aldrin landed on the moon. Michael Collins stayed in the command ship, orbiting the moon.
Houston, Tranquility Base here. The *Eagle* has landed.
Armstrong was the first human to step on the moon. This historic moment happened on July 20, 1969.
That's one small step for a man, one giant leap for mankind.

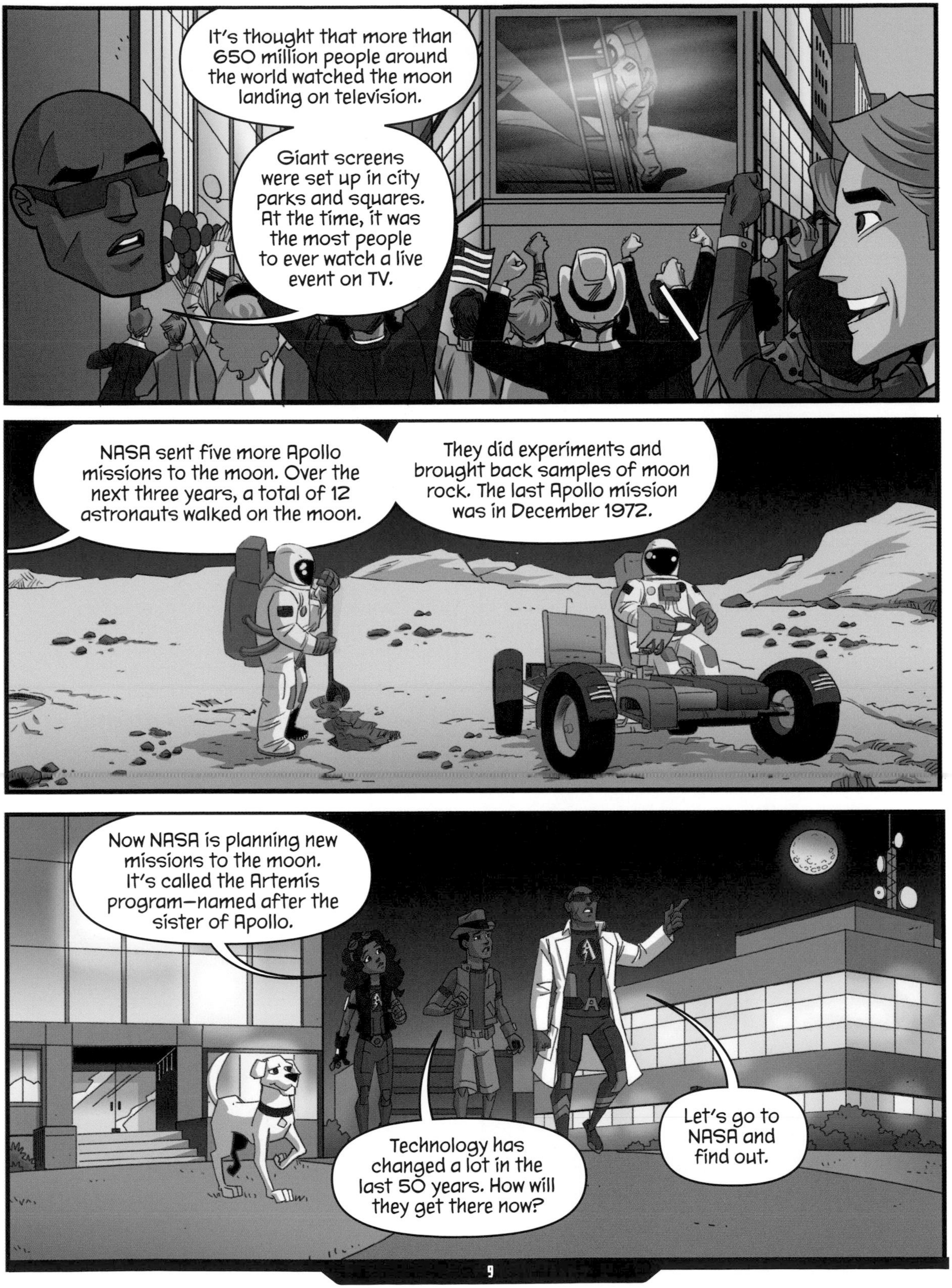
It's thought that more than 650 million people around the world watched the moon landing on television.
Giant screens were set up in city parks and squares. At the time, it was the most people to ever watch a live event on TV.
NASA sent five more Apollo missions to the moon. Over the next three years, a total of 12 astronauts walked on the moon.
They did experiments and brought back samples of moon rock. The last Apollo mission was in December 1972.
Now NASA is planning new missions to the moon. It's called the Artemis program—named after the sister of Apollo.
Technology has changed a lot in the last 50 years. How will they get there now?
Let's go to NASA and find out.

SECTION 2: *ROCKET POWER*

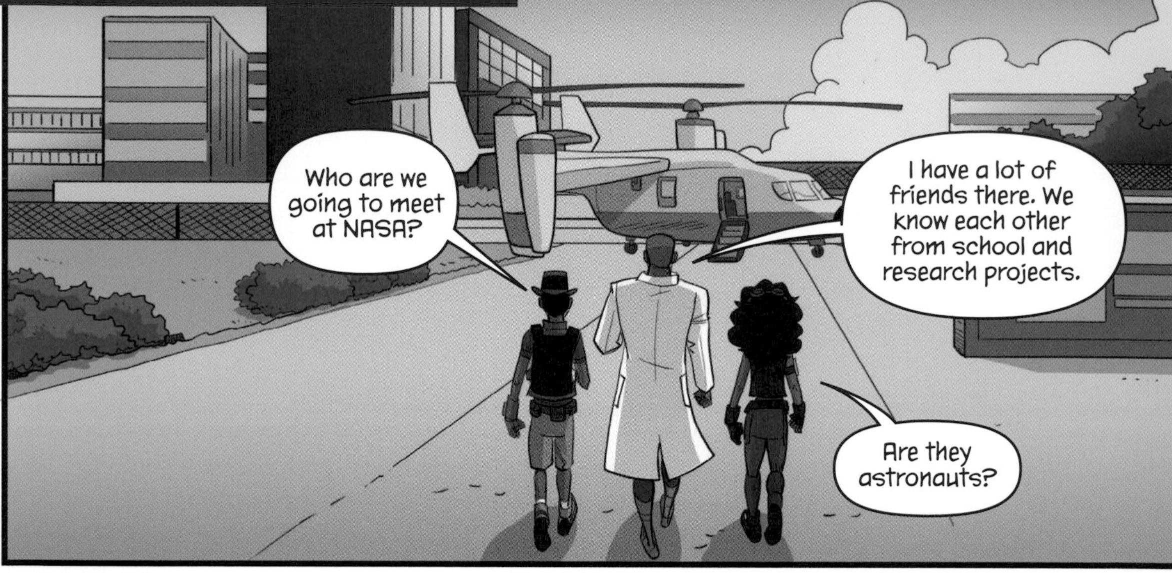

Who are we going to meet at NASA?
I have a lot of friends there. We know each other from school and research projects.
Are they astronauts?

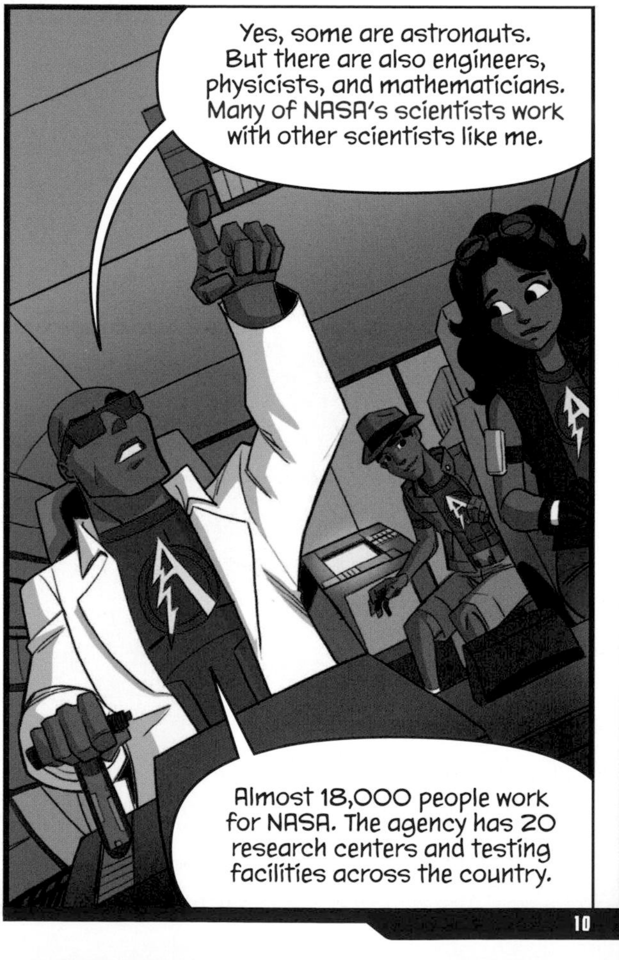

Yes, some are astronauts. But there are also engineers, physicists, and mathematicians. Many of NASA's scientists work with other scientists like me.
Almost 18,000 people work for NASA. The agency has 20 research centers and testing facilities across the country.

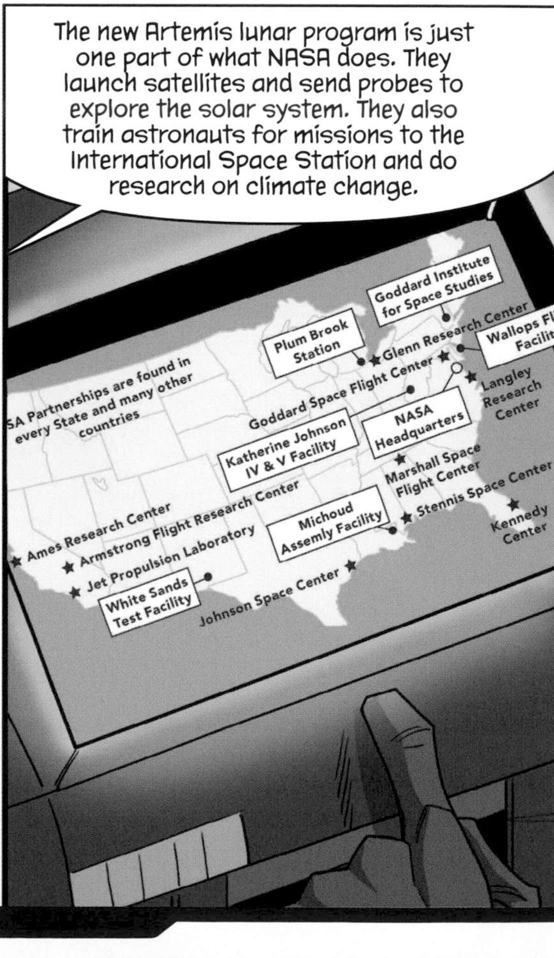

The new Artemis lunar program is just one part of what NASA does. They launch satellites and send probes to explore the solar system. They also train astronauts for missions to the International Space Station and do research on climate change.
Goddard Institute for Space Studies
Plum Brook Station
Glenn Research Center
Wallops Fli
Facility
Langley Research Center
SA Partnerships are found in every State and many other countries
Goddard Space Flight Center
NASA Headquarters
Katherine Johnson IV & V Facility
Marshall Space Flight Center
Stennis Space Center
Kennedy Center
Armstrong Flight Research Center
Ames Research Center
Michoud Assemly Facility
Jet Propulsion Laboratory
White Sands Test Facility
Johnson Space Center

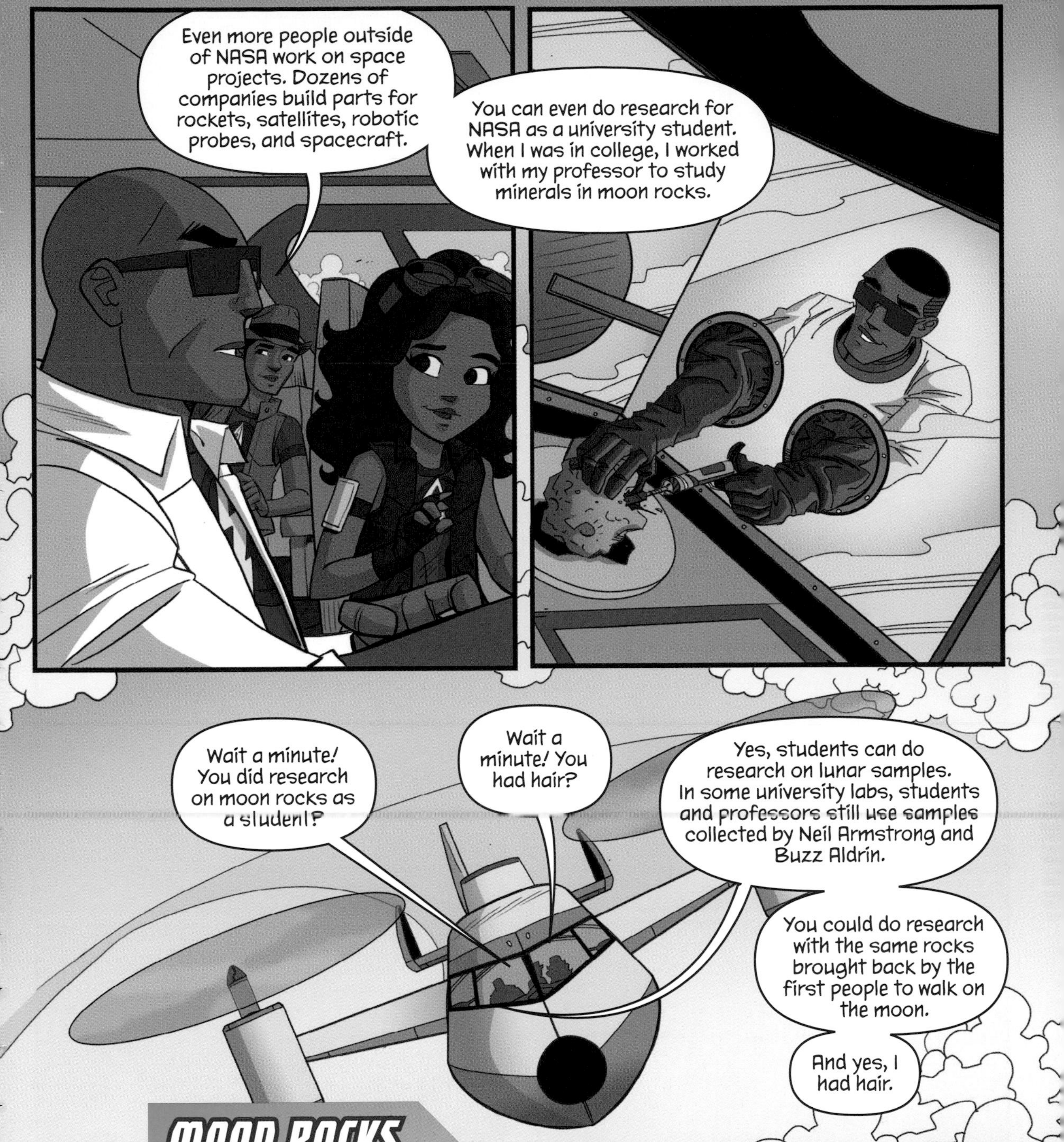
Even more people outside of NASA work on space projects. Dozens of companies build parts for rockets, satellites, robotic probes, and spacecraft.
You can even do research for NASA as a university student. When I was in college, I worked with my professor to study minerals in moon rocks.
Wait a minute! You did research on moon rocks as a student?
Wait a minute! You had hair?
Yes, students can do research on lunar samples. In some university labs, students and professors still use samples collected by Neil Armstrong and Buzz Aldrin.
You could do research with the same rocks brought back by the first people to walk on the moon.
And yes, I had hair.

MOON ROCKS

The Apollo missions brought back 2,196 samples of lunar rocks and soil. Together the samples weigh a total of 842 pounds (382 kilograms). Most of the rock samples are still at NASA. But many are used for research at other labs. Some are on display in museums.

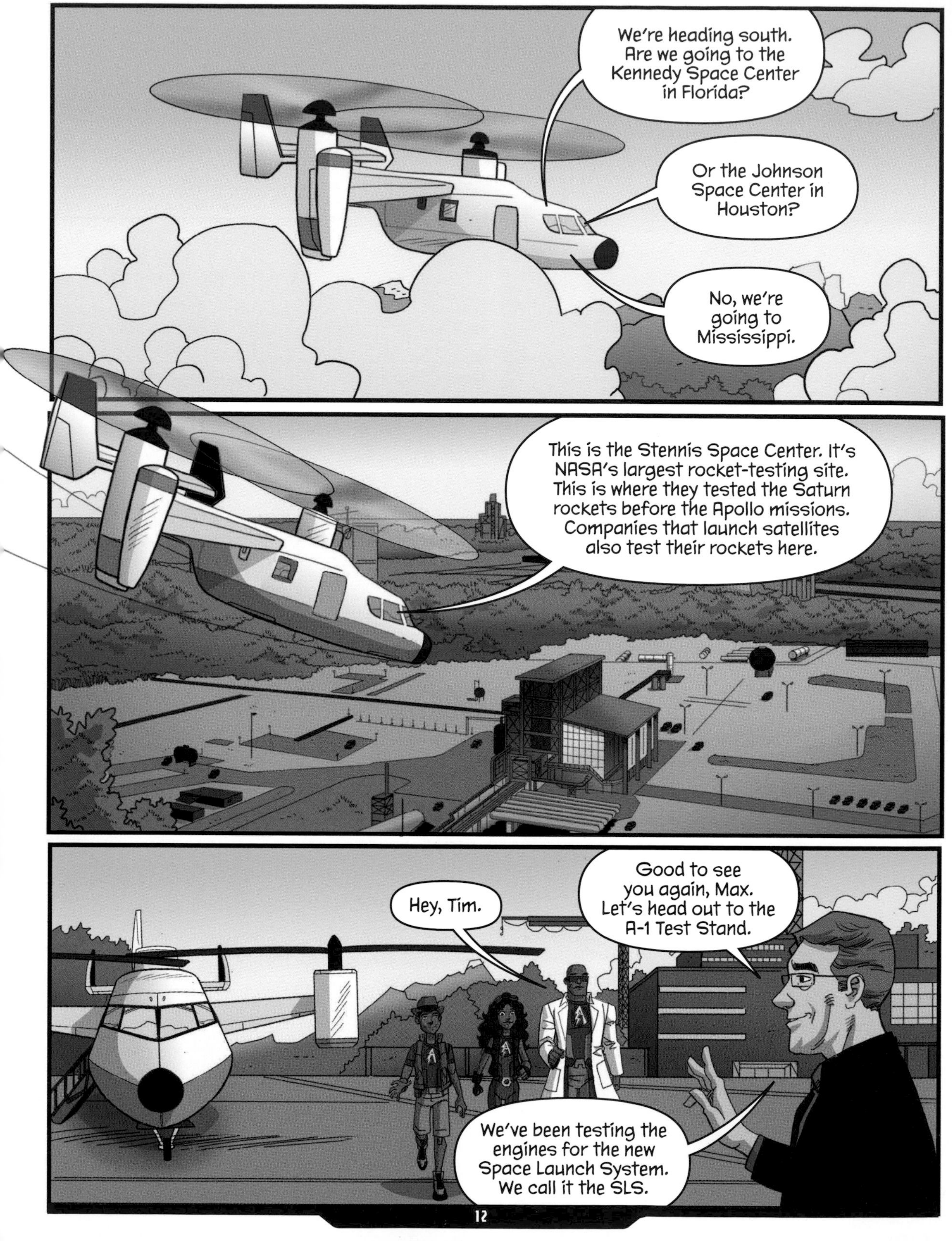
We're heading south. Are we going to the Kennedy Space Center in Florida?
Or the Johnson Space Center in Houston?
No, we're going to Mississippi.
This is the Stennis Space Center. It's NASA's largest rocket-testing site. This is where they tested the Saturn rockets before the Apollo missions. Companies that launch satellites also test their rockets here.
Hey, Tim.
Good to see you again, Max. Let's head out to the A-1 Test Stand.
We've been testing the engines for the new Space Launch System. We call it the SLS.

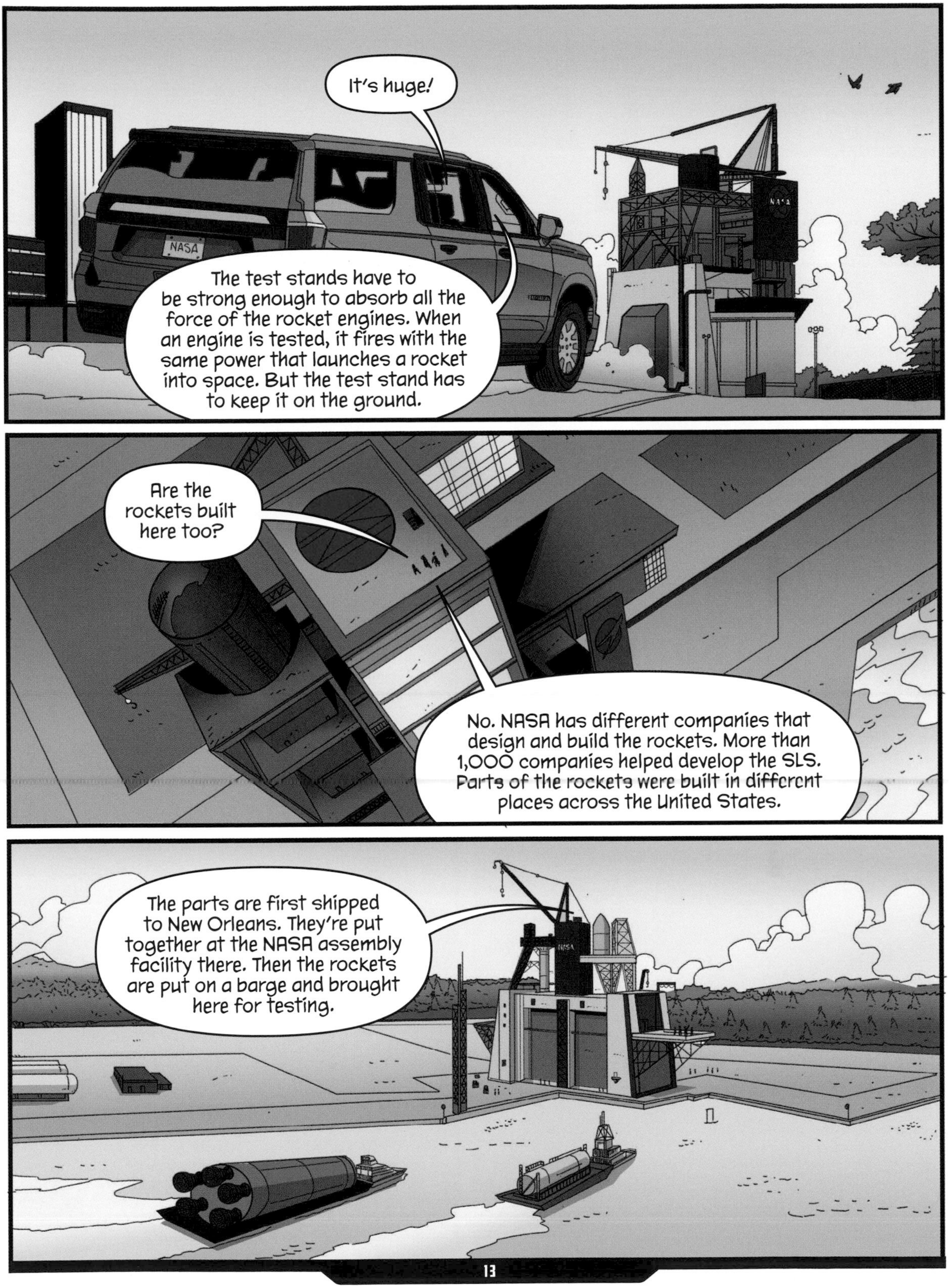
It's huge!
The test stands have to be strong enough to absorb all the force of the rocket engines. When an engine is tested, it fires with the same power that launches a rocket into space. But the test stand has to keep it on the ground.
NASA
Are the rockets built here too?
No. NASA has different companies that design and build the rockets. More than 1,000 companies helped develop the SLS. Parts of the rockets were built in different places across the United States.
The parts are first shipped to New Orleans. They're put together at the NASA assembly facility there. Then the rockets are put on a barge and brought here for testing.

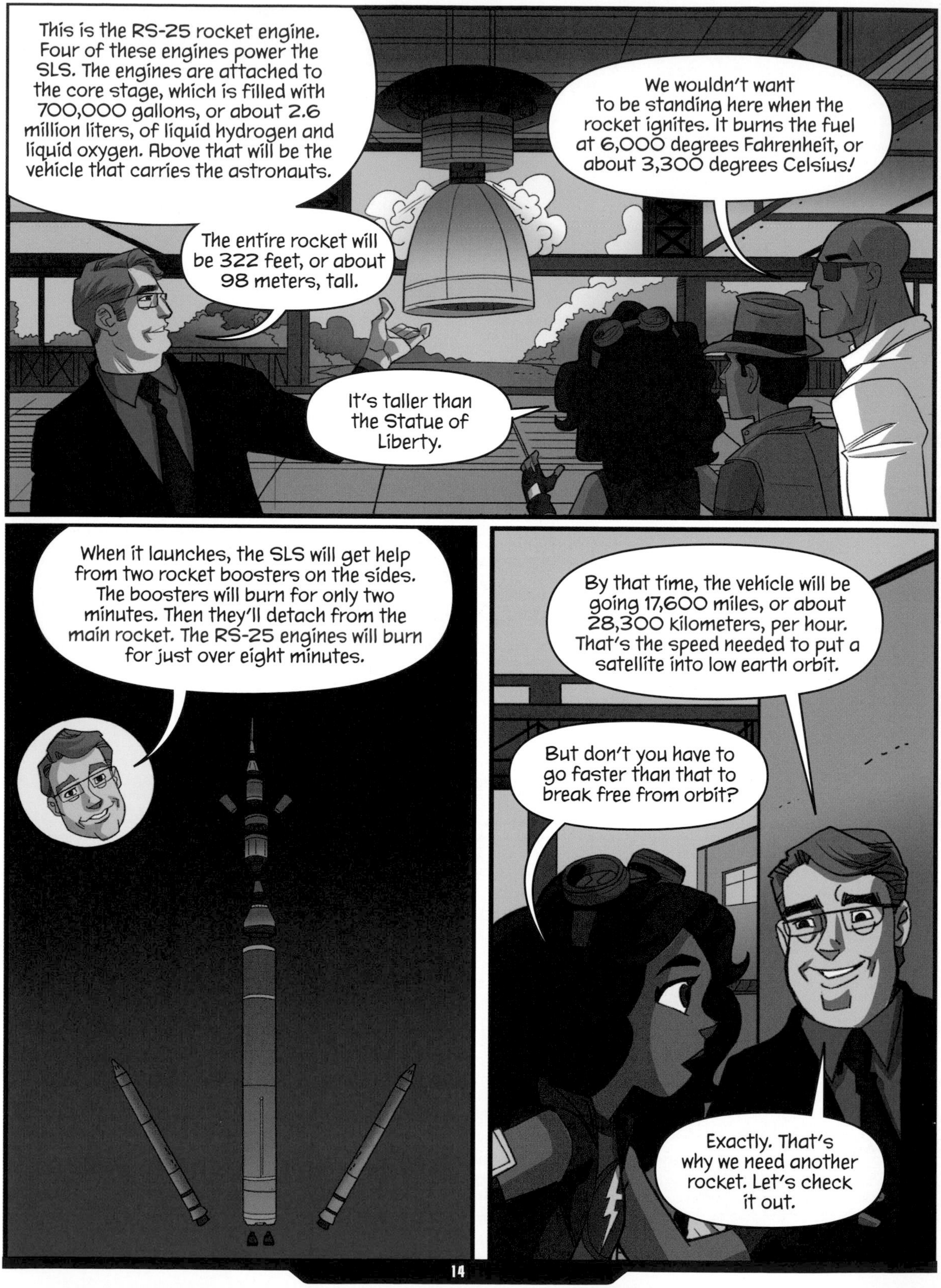
This is the RS-25 rocket engine. Four of these engines power the SLS. The engines are attached to the core stage, which is filled with 700,000 gallons, or about 2.6 million liters, of liquid hydrogen and liquid oxygen. Above that will be the vehicle that carries the astronauts.
The entire rocket will be 322 feet, or about 98 meters, tall.
We wouldn't want to be standing here when the rocket ignites. It burns the fuel at 6,000 degrees Fahrenheit, or about 3,300 degrees Celsius!
It's taller than the Statue of Liberty.
When it launches, the SLS will get help from two rocket boosters on the sides. The boosters will burn for only two minutes. Then they'll detach from the main rocket. The RS-25 engines will burn for just over eight minutes.
By that time, the vehicle will be going 17,600 miles, or about 28,300 kilometers, per hour. That's the speed needed to put a satellite into low earth orbit.
But don't you have to go faster than that to break free from orbit?
Exactly. That's why we need another rocket. Let's check it out.

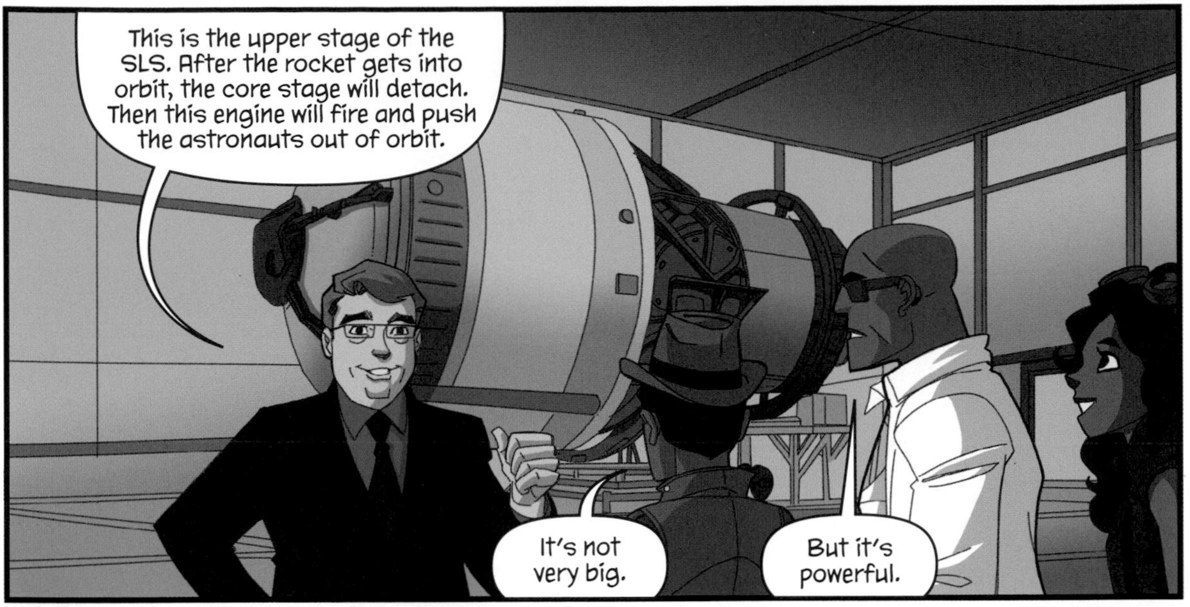
This is the upper stage of the SLS. After the rocket gets into orbit, the core stage will detach. Then this engine will fire and push the astronauts out of orbit.
It's not very big.
But it's powerful.

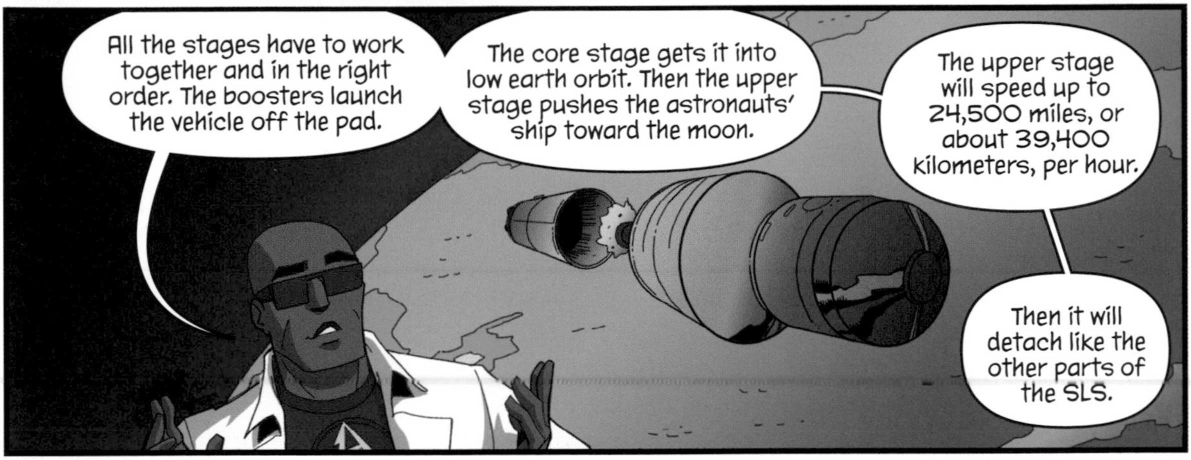
All the stages have to work together and in the right order. The boosters launch the vehicle off the pad.
The core stage gets it into low earth orbit. Then the upper stage pushes the astronauts' ship toward the moon.
The upper stage will speed up to 24,500 miles, or about 39,400 kilometers, per hour.
Then it will detach like the other parts of the SLS.

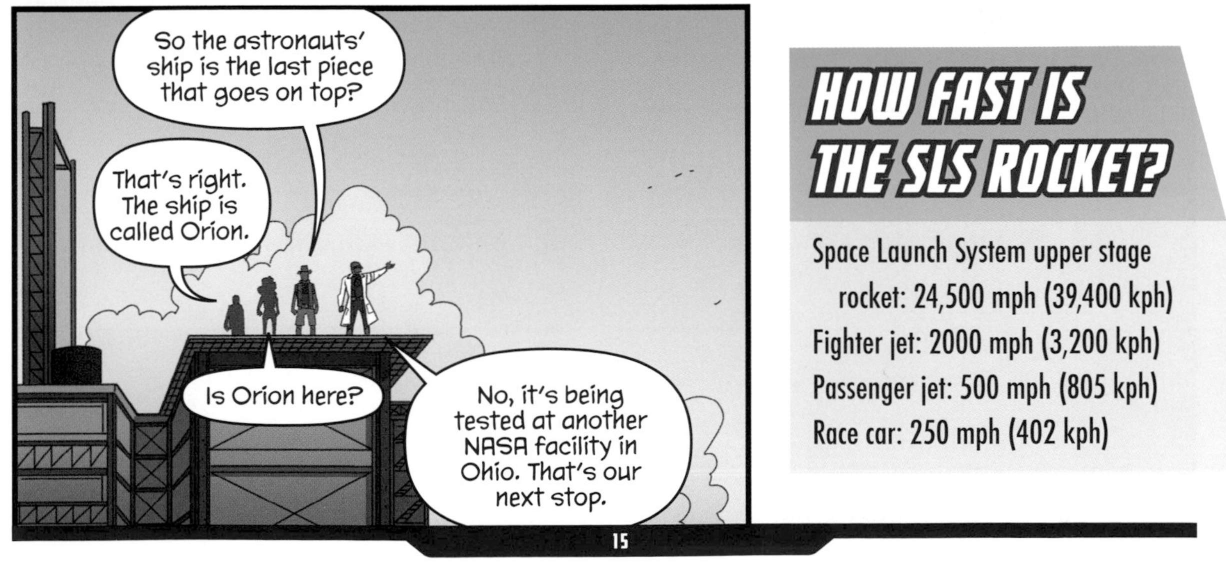
So the astronauts' ship is the last piece that goes on top?
That's right. The ship is called Orion.
Is Orion here?
No, it's being tested at another NASA facility in Ohio. That's our next stop.

HOW FAST IS THE SLS ROCKET?

Space Launch System upper stage rocket: 24,500 mph (39,400 kph)

Fighter jet: 2000 mph (3,200 kph)

Passenger jet: 500 mph (805 kph)

Race car: 250 mph (402 kph)

SECTION 3: TRAVELING THROUGH SPACE

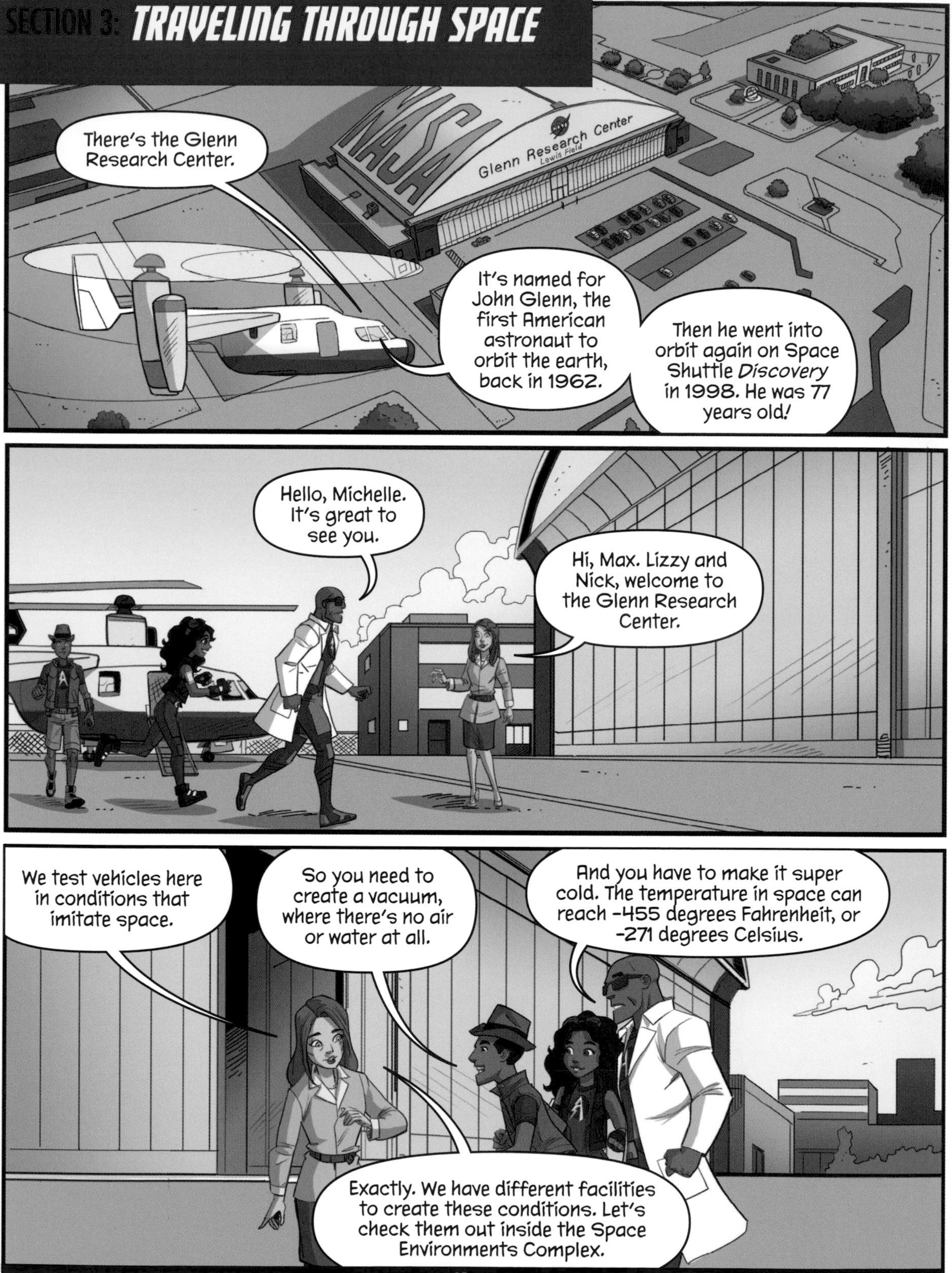

There's the Glenn Research Center.
NASA
Glenn Research Center
Lewis Field
It's named for John Glenn, the first American astronaut to orbit the earth, back in 1962.
Then he went into orbit again on Space Shuttle *Discovery* in 1998. He was 77 years old!
Hello, Michelle. It's great to see you.
Hi, Max. Lizzy and Nick, welcome to the Glenn Research Center.
We test vehicles here in conditions that imitate space.
So you need to create a vacuum, where there's no air or water at all.
And you have to make it super cold. The temperature in space can reach –455 degrees Fahrenheit, or –271 degrees Celsius.
Exactly. We have different facilities to create these conditions. Let's check them out inside the Space Environments Complex.

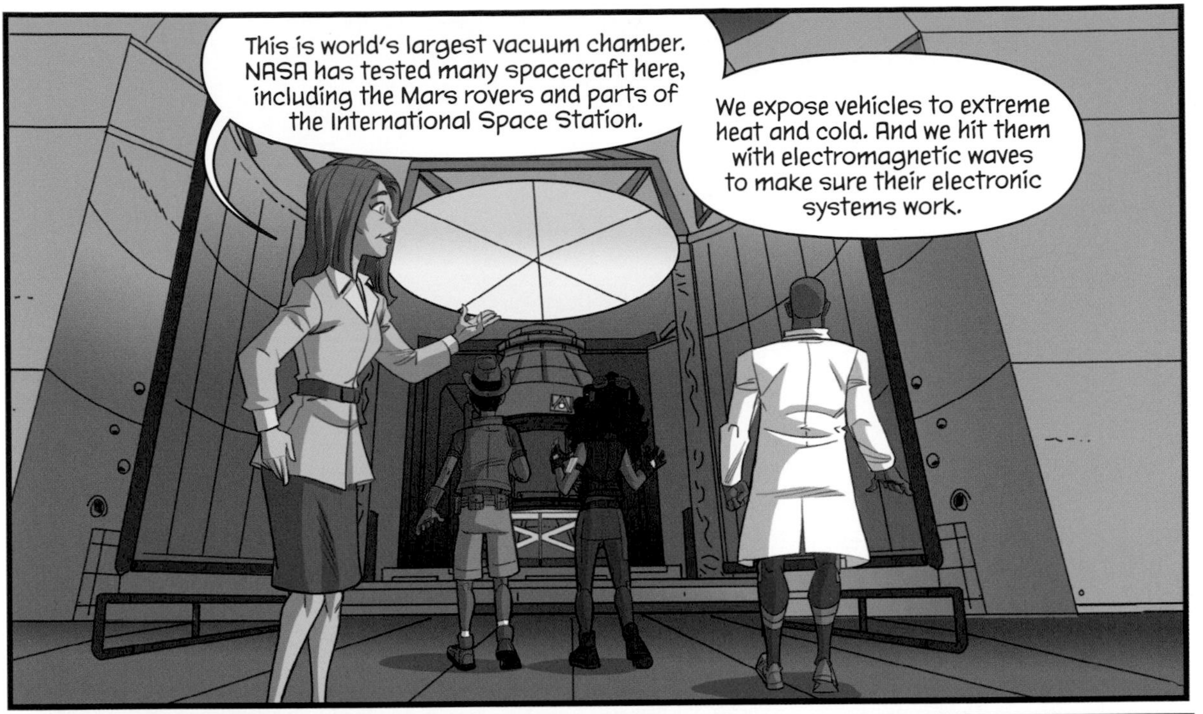
This is world's largest vacuum chamber. NASA has tested many spacecraft here, including the Mars rovers and parts of the International Space Station.
We expose vehicles to extreme heat and cold. And we hit them with electromagnetic waves to make sure their electronic systems work.

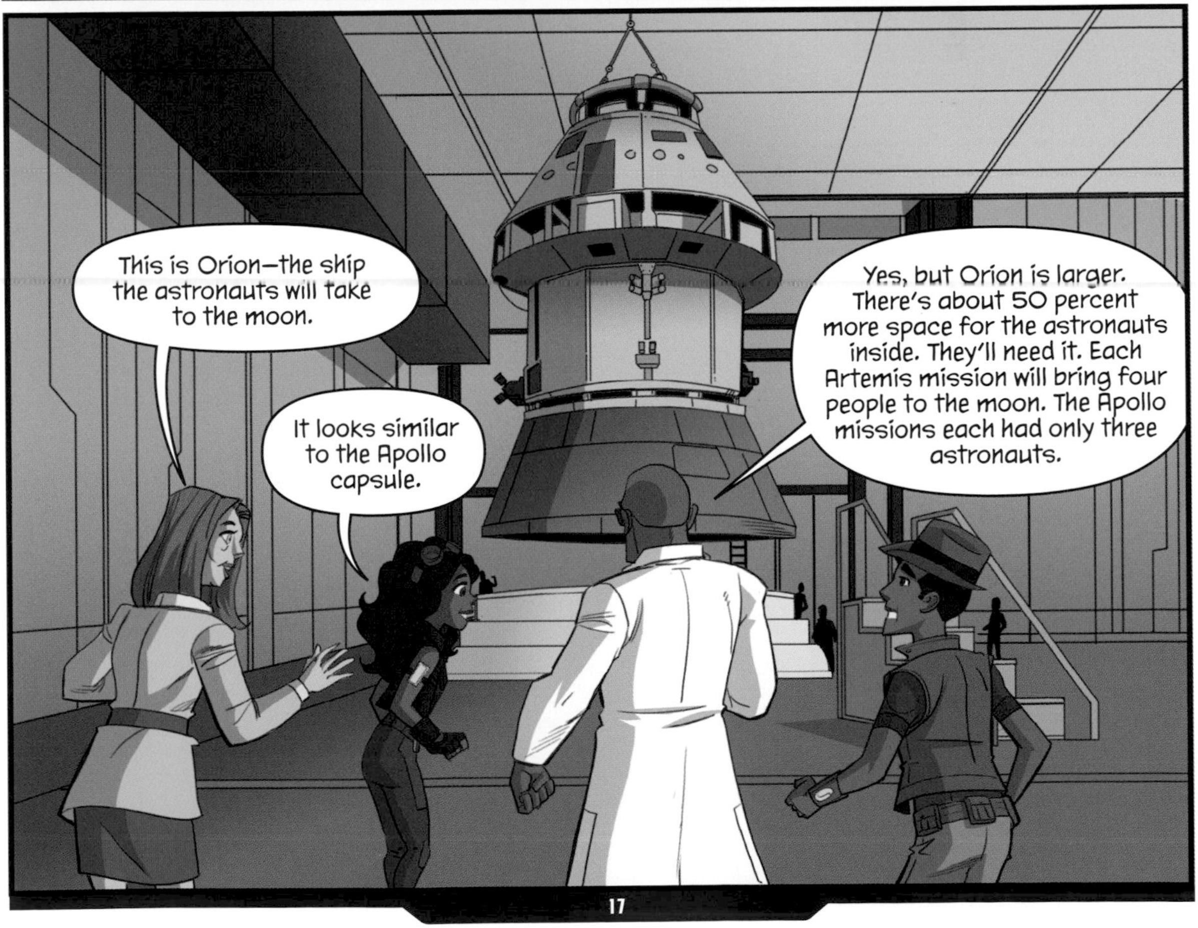
This is Orion—the ship the astronauts will take to the moon.
It looks similar to the Apollo capsule.
Yes, but Orion is larger. There's about 50 percent more space for the astronauts inside. They'll need it. Each Artemis mission will bring four people to the moon. The Apollo missions each had only three astronauts.

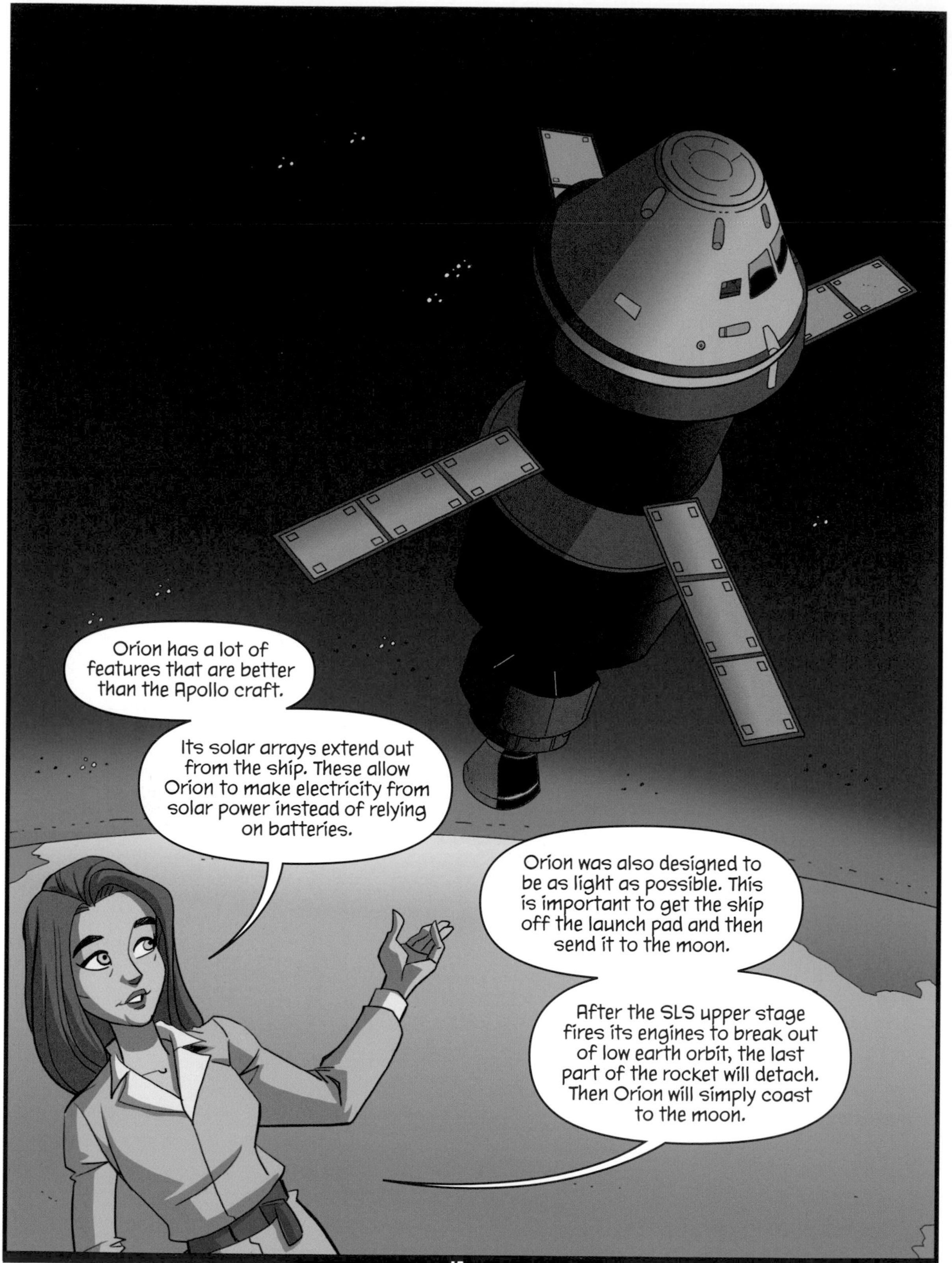
Orion has a lot of features that are better than the Apollo craft.
Its solar arrays extend out from the ship. These allow Orion to make electricity from solar power instead of relying on batteries.
Orion was also designed to be as light as possible. This is important to get the ship off the launch pad and then send it to the moon.
After the SLS upper stage fires its engines to break out of low earth orbit, the last part of the rocket will detach. Then Orion will simply coast to the moon.

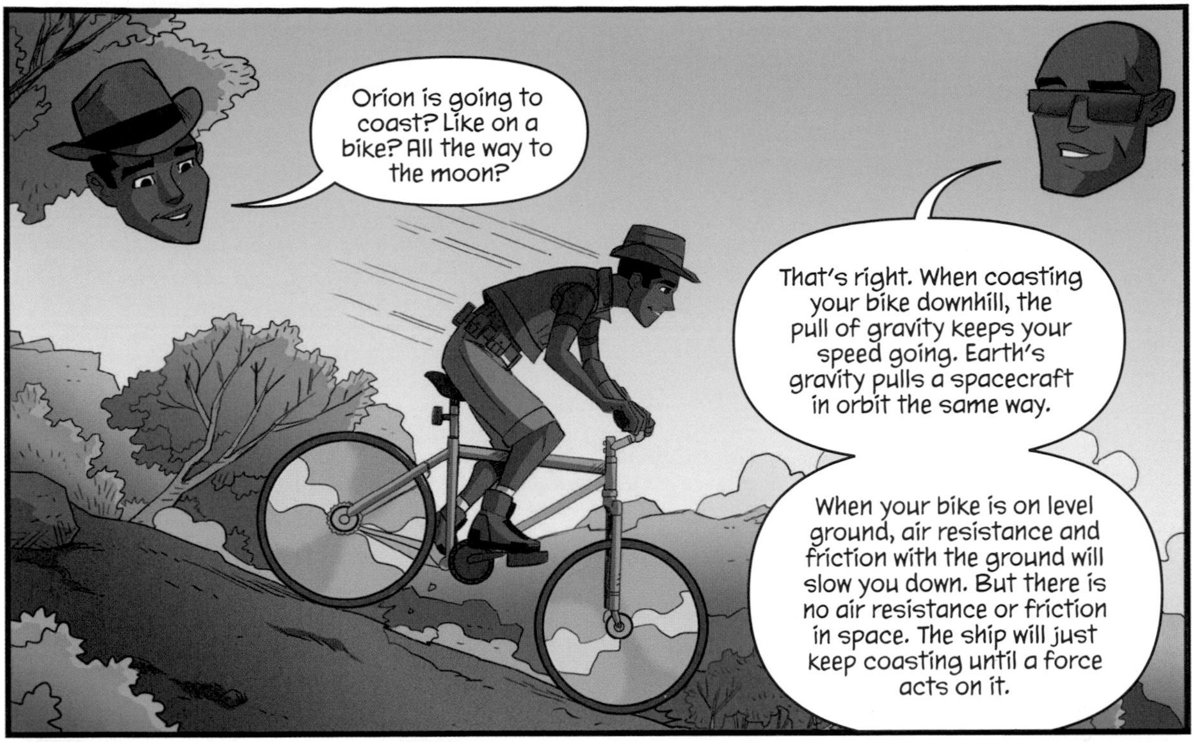
Orion is going to coast? Like on a bike? All the way to the moon?
That's right. When coasting your bike downhill, the pull of gravity keeps your speed going. Earth's gravity pulls a spacecraft in orbit the same way.
When your bike is on level ground, air resistance and friction with the ground will slow you down. But there is no air resistance or friction in space. The ship will just keep coasting until a force acts on it.

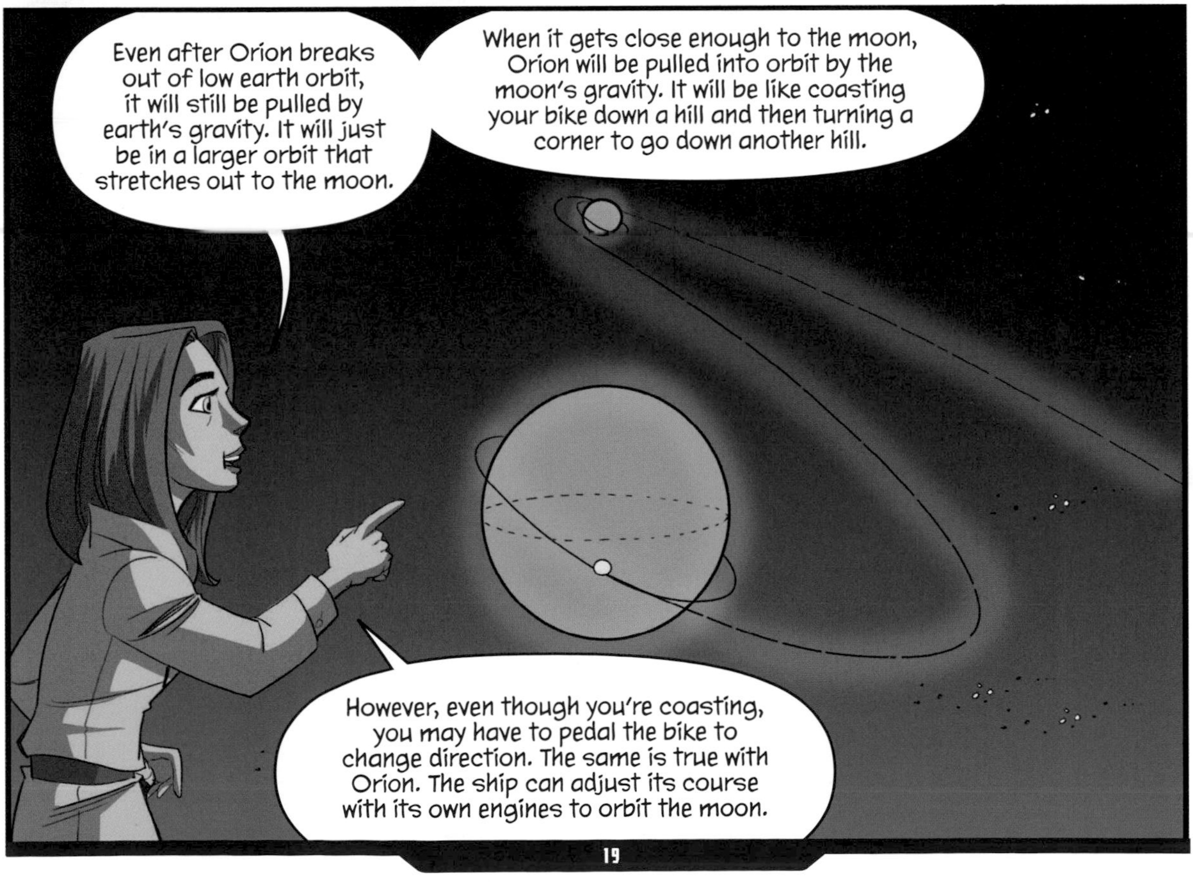
Even after Orion breaks out of low earth orbit, it will still be pulled by earth's gravity. It will just be in a larger orbit that stretches out to the moon.
When it gets close enough to the moon, Orion will be pulled into orbit by the moon's gravity. It will be like coasting your bike down a hill and then turning a corner to go down another hill.
However, even though you're coasting, you may have to pedal the bike to change direction. The same is true with Orion. The ship can adjust its course with its own engines to orbit the moon.

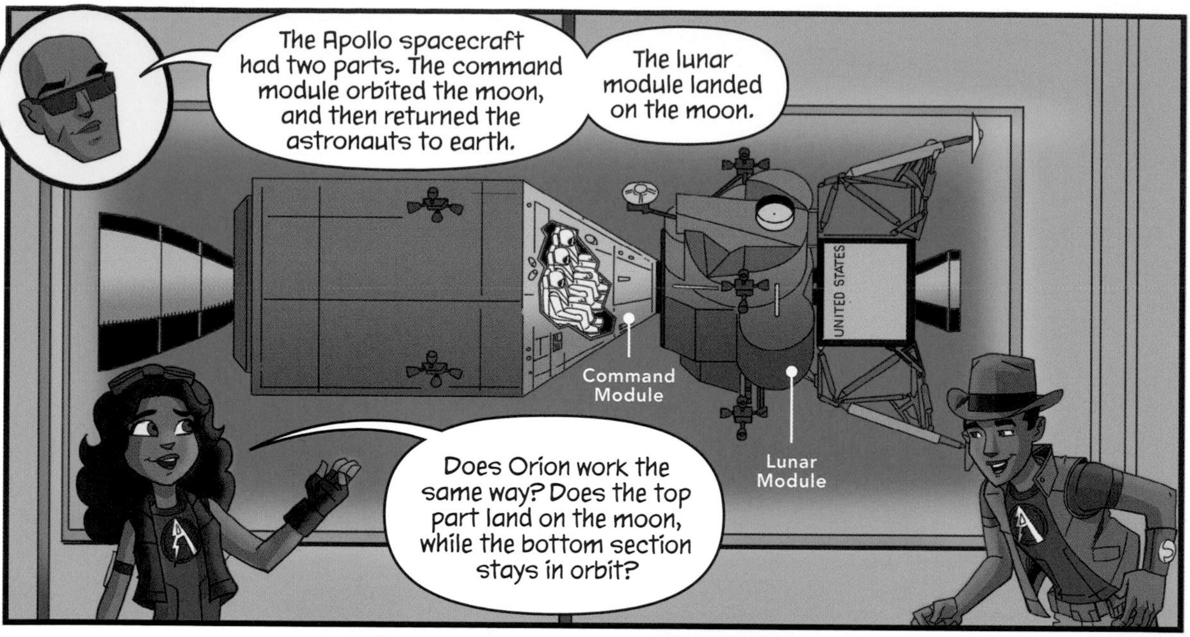
The Apollo spacecraft had two parts. The command module orbited the moon, and then returned the astronauts to earth.
The lunar module landed on the moon.
UNITED STATES
Command Module
Lunar Module
Does Orion work the same way? Does the top part land on the moon, while the bottom section stays in orbit?

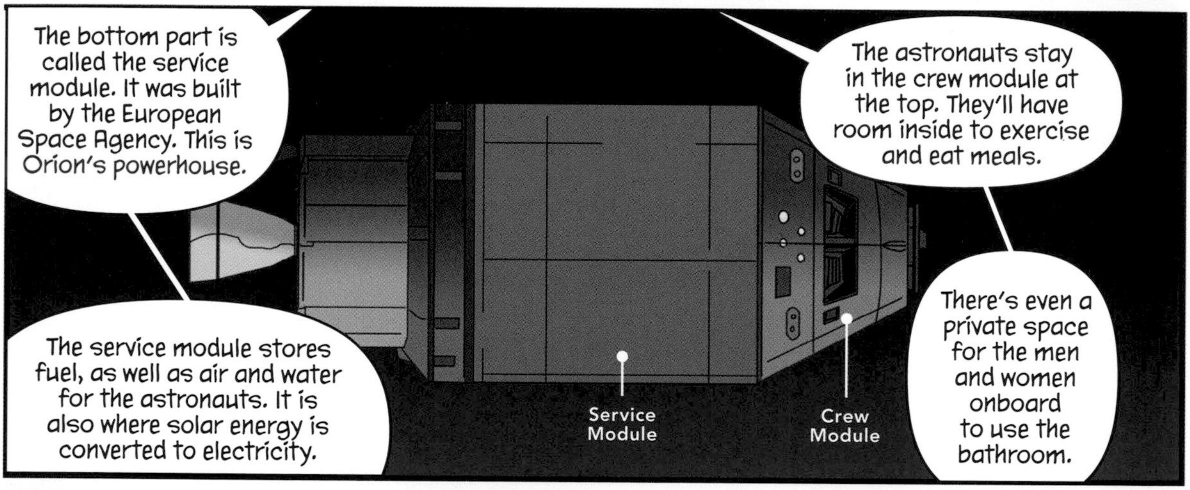
The bottom part is called the service module. It was built by the European Space Agency. This is Orion's powerhouse.
The astronauts stay in the crew module at the top. They'll have room inside to exercise and eat meals.
The service module stores fuel, as well as air and water for the astronauts. It is also where solar energy is converted to electricity.
Service Module
Crew Module
There's even a private space for the men and women onboard to use the bathroom.

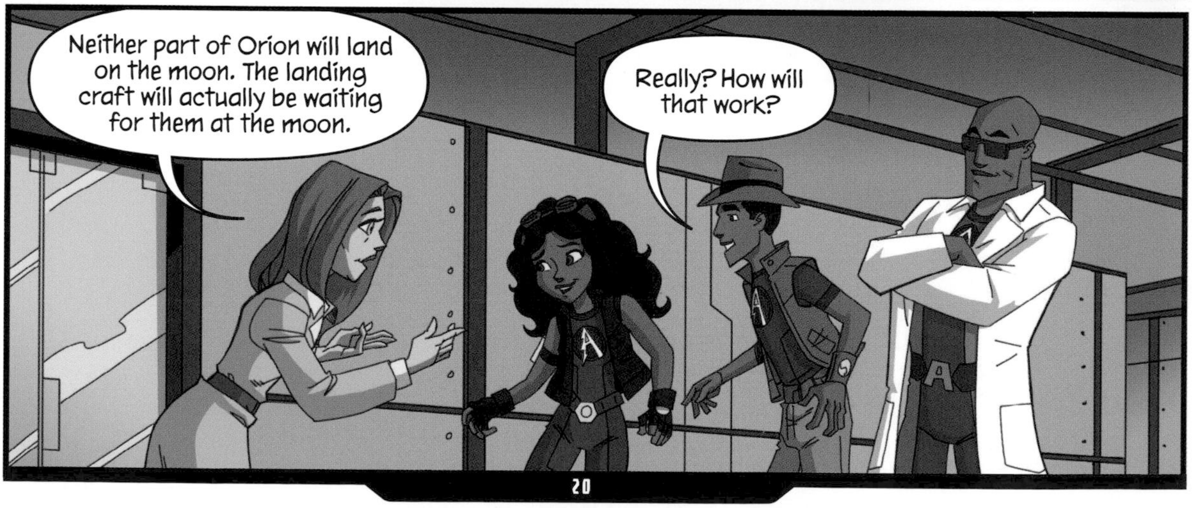
Neither part of Orion will land on the moon. The landing craft will actually be waiting for them at the moon.
Really? How will that work?

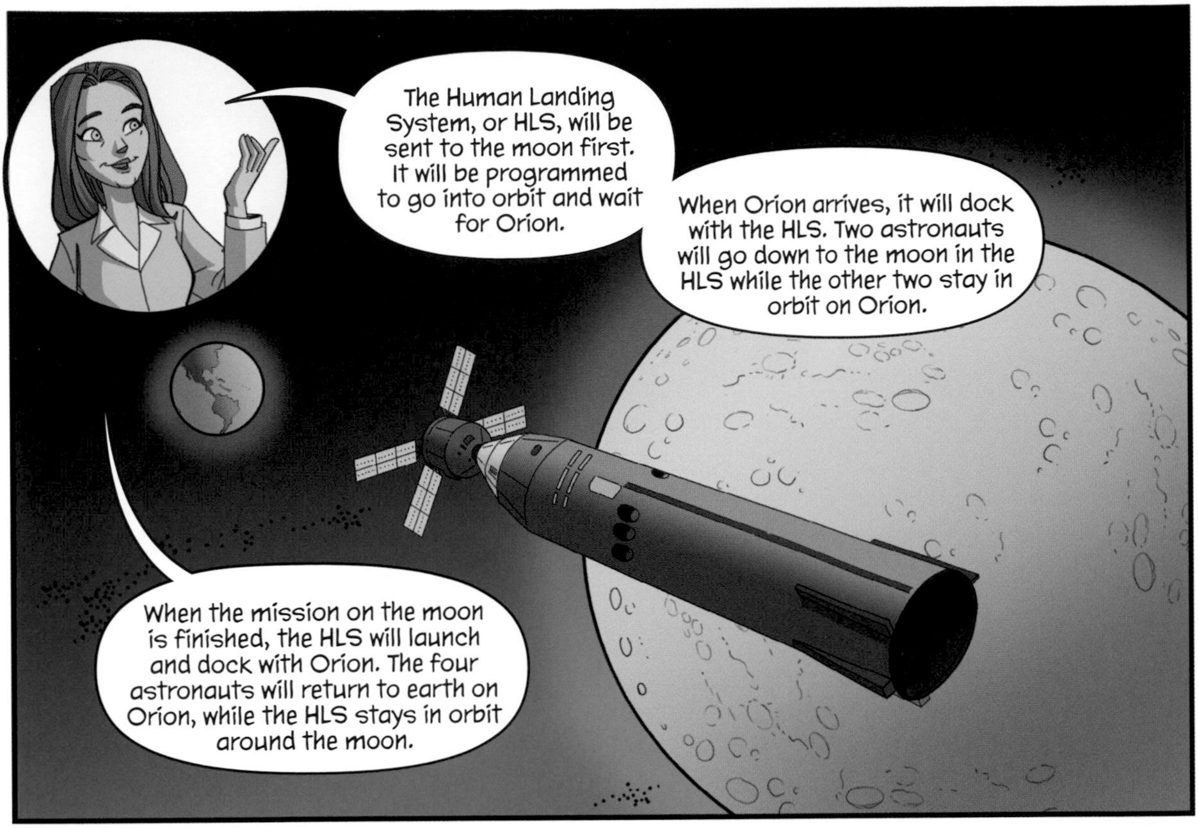
The Human Landing System, or HLS, will be sent to the moon first. It will be programmed to go into orbit and wait for Orion.
When Orion arrives, it will dock with the HLS. Two astronauts will go down to the moon in the HLS while the other two stay in orbit on Orion.
When the mission on the moon is finished, the HLS will launch and dock with Orion. The four astronauts will return to earth on Orion, while the HLS stays in orbit around the moon.

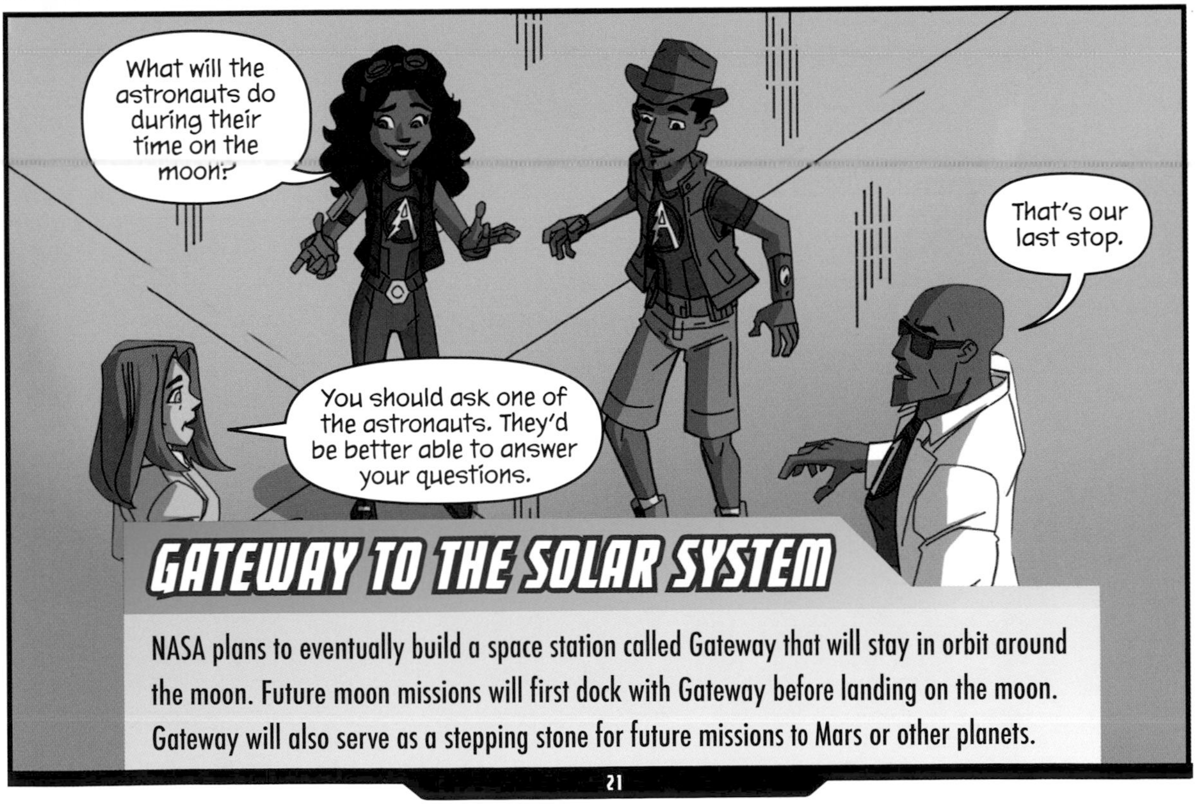
What will the astronauts do during their time on the moon?
That's our last stop.
You should ask one of the astronauts. They'd be better able to answer your questions.

GATEWAY TO THE SOLAR SYSTEM

NASA plans to eventually build a space station called Gateway that will stay in orbit around the moon. Future moon missions will first dock with Gateway before landing on the moon. Gateway will also serve as a stepping stone for future missions to Mars or other planets.

SECTION 4: BACK TO THE MOON

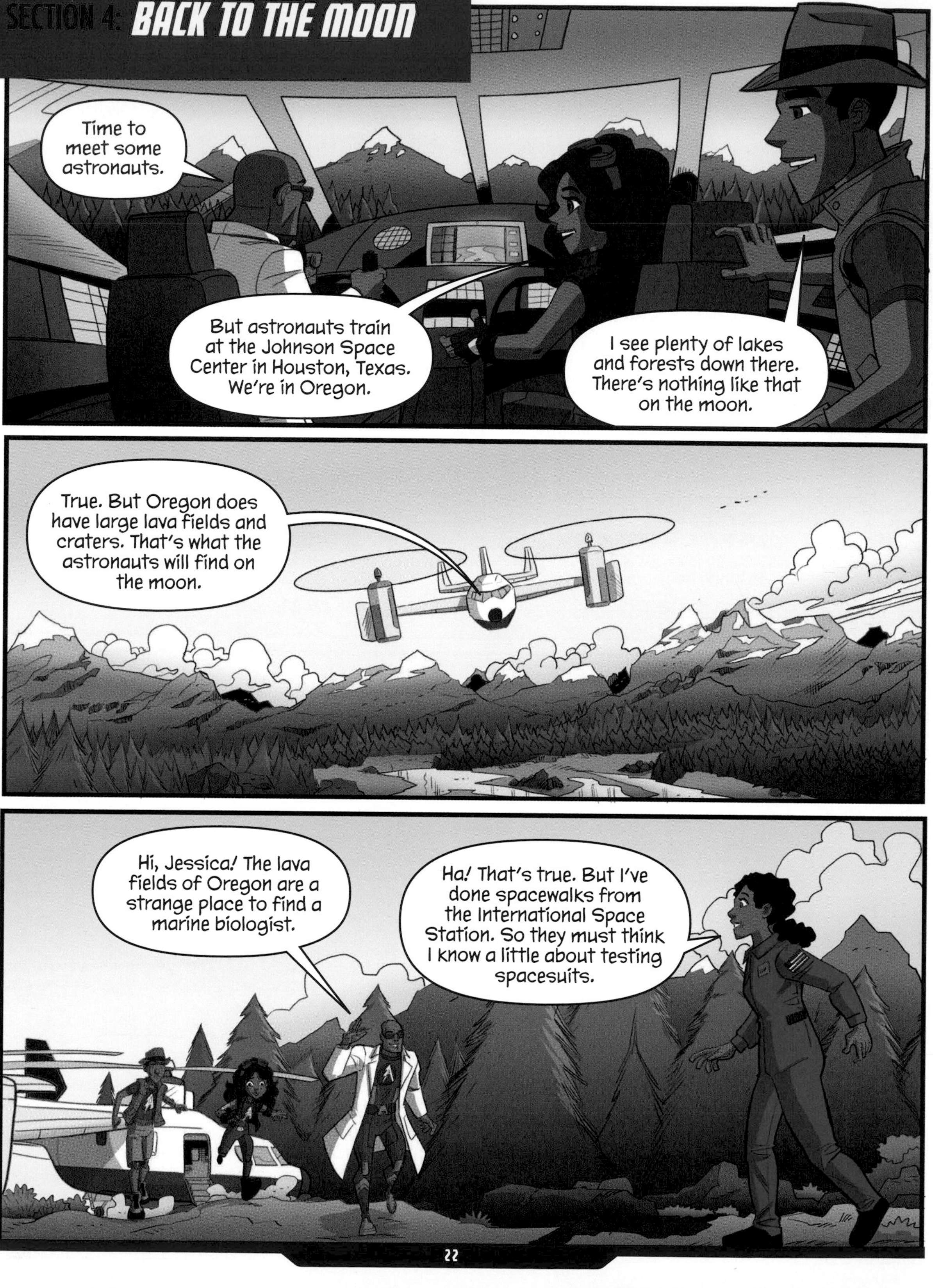
Time to meet some astronauts.
But astronauts train at the Johnson Space Center in Houston, Texas. We're in Oregon.
I see plenty of lakes and forests down there. There's nothing like that on the moon.
True. But Oregon does have large lava fields and craters. That's what the astronauts will find on the moon.
Hi, Jessica! The lava fields of Oregon are a strange place to find a marine biologist.
Ha! That's true. But I've done spacewalks from the International Space Station. So they must think I know a little about testing spacesuits.

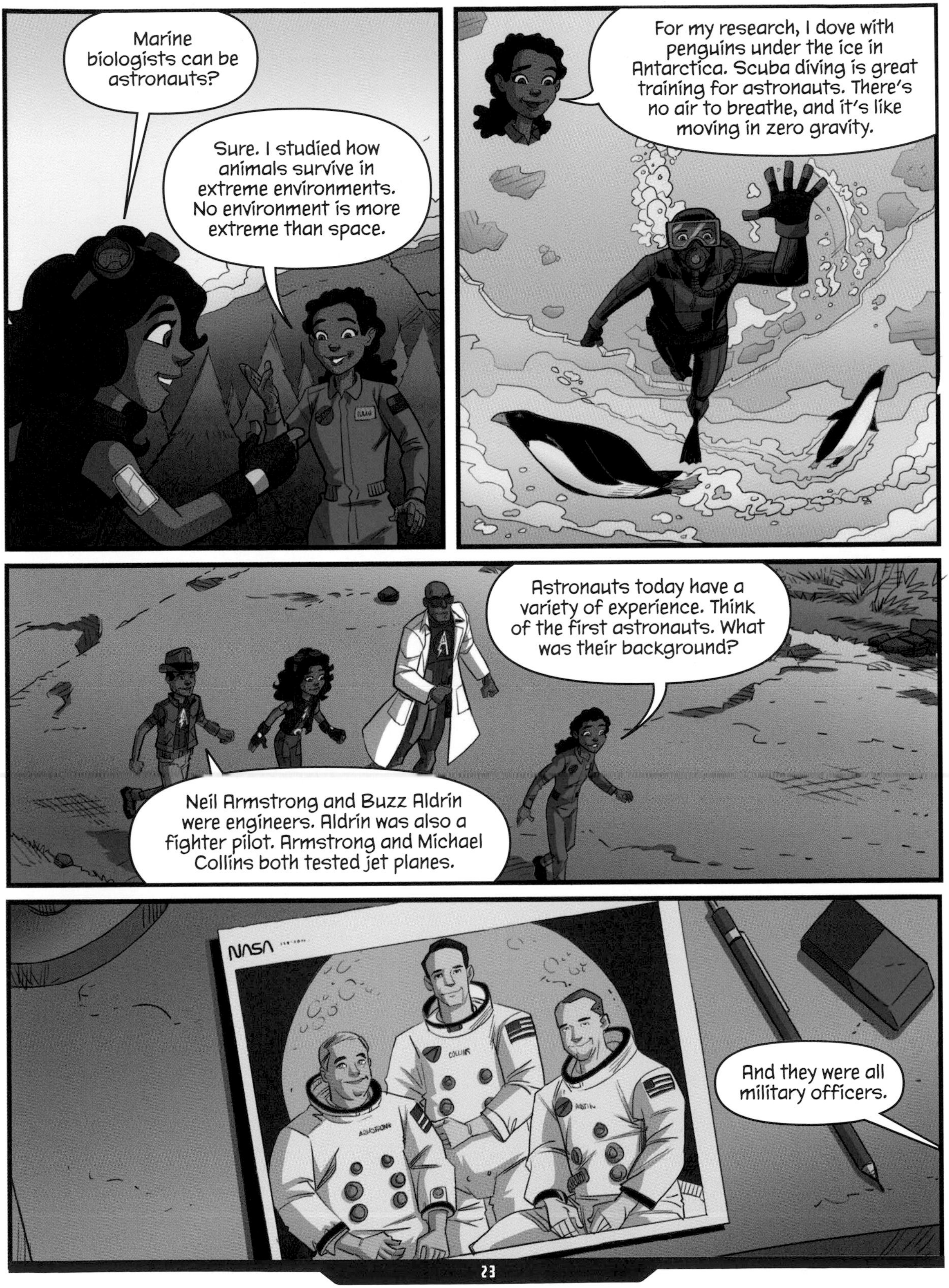
Marine biologists can be astronauts?
Sure. I studied how animals survive in extreme environments. No environment is more extreme than space.
For my research, I dove with penguins under the ice in Antarctica. Scuba diving is great training for astronauts. There's no air to breathe, and it's like moving in zero gravity.
Astronauts today have a variety of experience. Think of the first astronauts. What was their background?
Neil Armstrong and Buzz Aldrin were engineers. Aldrin was also a fighter pilot. Armstrong and Michael Collins both tested jet planes.
NASA
COLLINS
ARMSTRONG
ALDRIN
And they were all military officers.

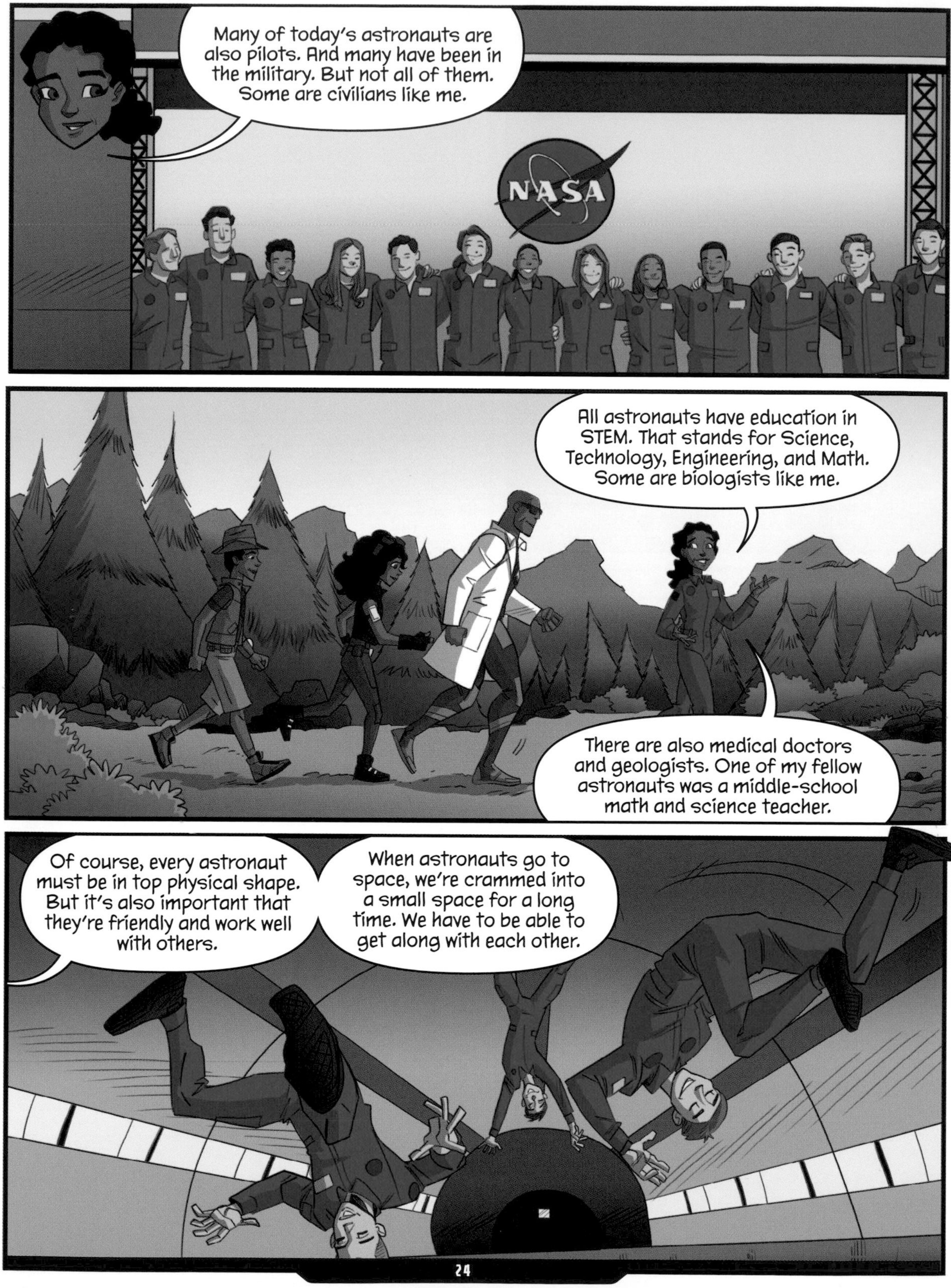
Many of today's astronauts are also pilots. And many have been in the military. But not all of them. Some are civilians like me.
NASA
All astronauts have education in STEM. That stands for Science, Technology, Engineering, and Math. Some are biologists like me.
There are also medical doctors and geologists. One of my fellow astronauts was a middle-school math and science teacher.
Of course, every astronaut must be in top physical shape. But it's also important that they're friendly and work well with others.
When astronauts go to space, we're crammed into a small space for a long time. We have to be able to get along with each other.

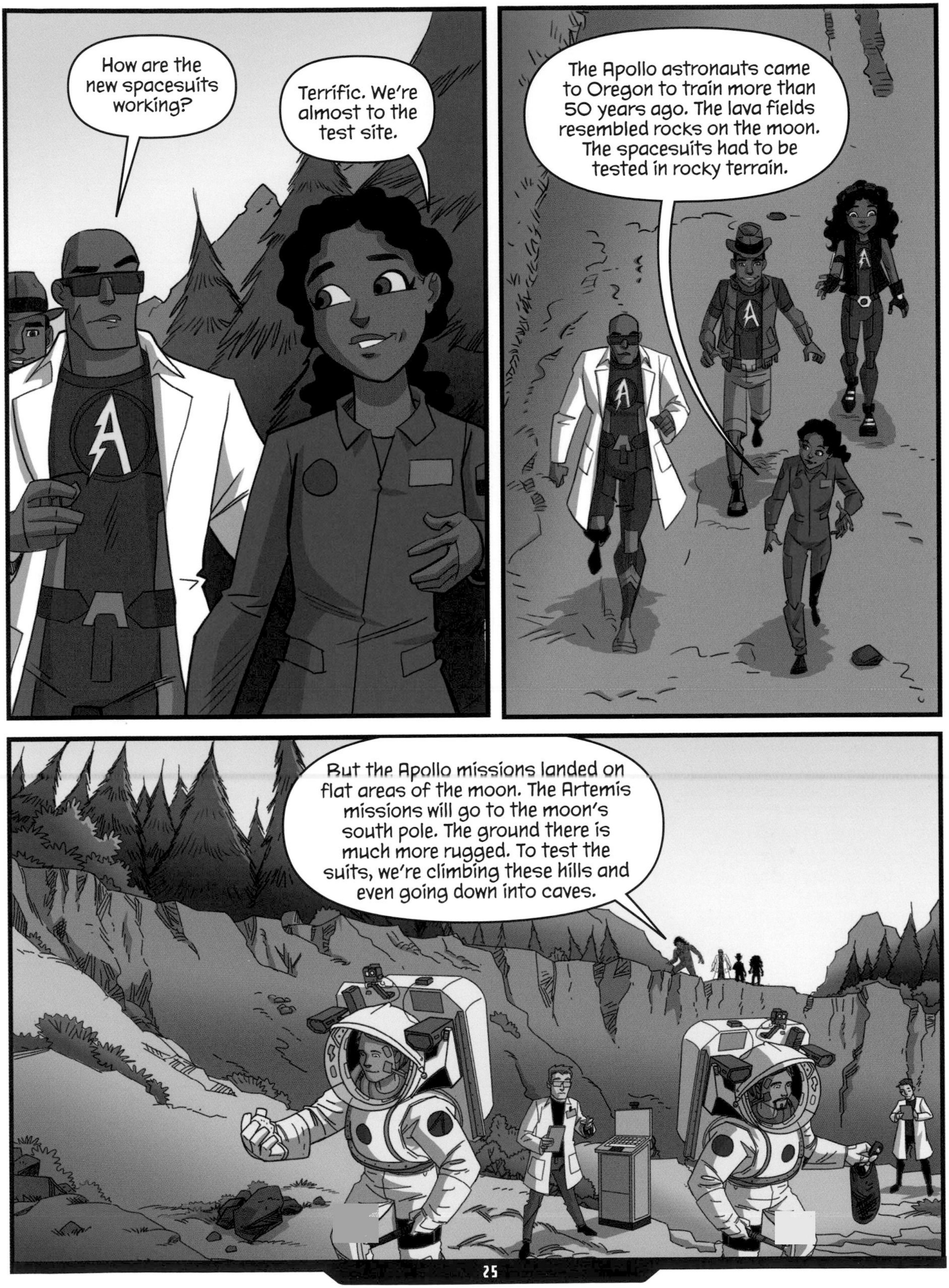
How are the new spacesuits working?
Terrific. We're almost to the test site.
The Apollo astronauts came to Oregon to train more than 50 years ago. The lava fields resembled rocks on the moon. The spacesuits had to be tested in rocky terrain.
But the Apollo missions landed on flat areas of the moon. The Artemis missions will go to the moon's south pole. The ground there is much more rugged. To test the suits, we're climbing these hills and even going down into caves.

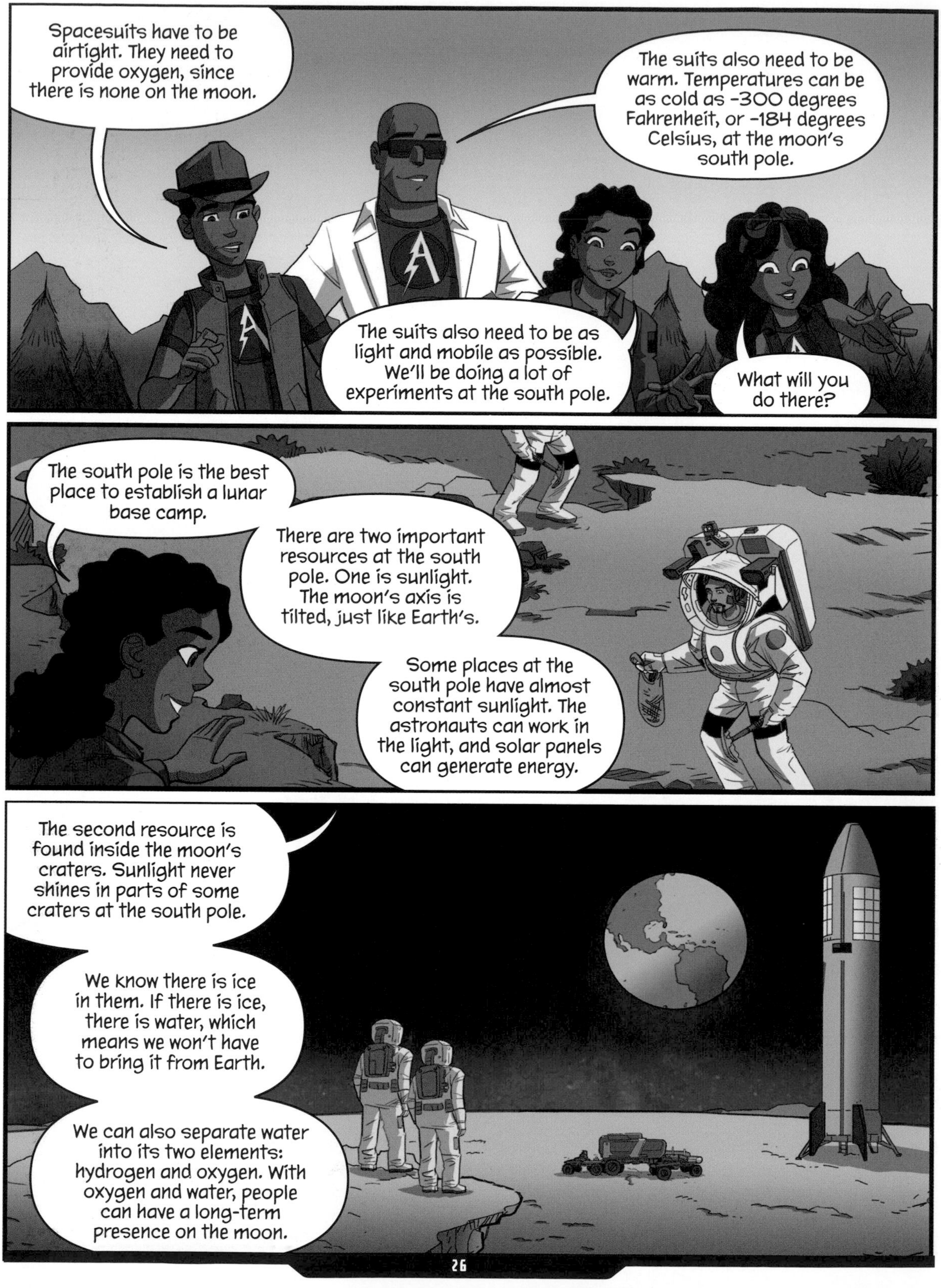
Spacesuits have to be airtight. They need to provide oxygen, since there is none on the moon.
The suits also need to be warm. Temperatures can be as cold as -300 degrees Fahrenheit, or -184 degrees Celsius, at the moon's south pole.
The suits also need to be as light and mobile as possible. We'll be doing a lot of experiments at the south pole.
What will you do there?
The south pole is the best place to establish a lunar base camp.
There are two important resources at the south pole. One is sunlight. The moon's axis is tilted, just like Earth's.
Some places at the south pole have almost constant sunlight. The astronauts can work in the light, and solar panels can generate energy.
The second resource is found inside the moon's craters. Sunlight never shines in parts of some craters at the south pole.
We know there is ice in them. If there is ice, there is water, which means we won't have to bring it from Earth.
We can also separate water into its two elements: hydrogen and oxygen. With oxygen and water, people can have a long-term presence on the moon.

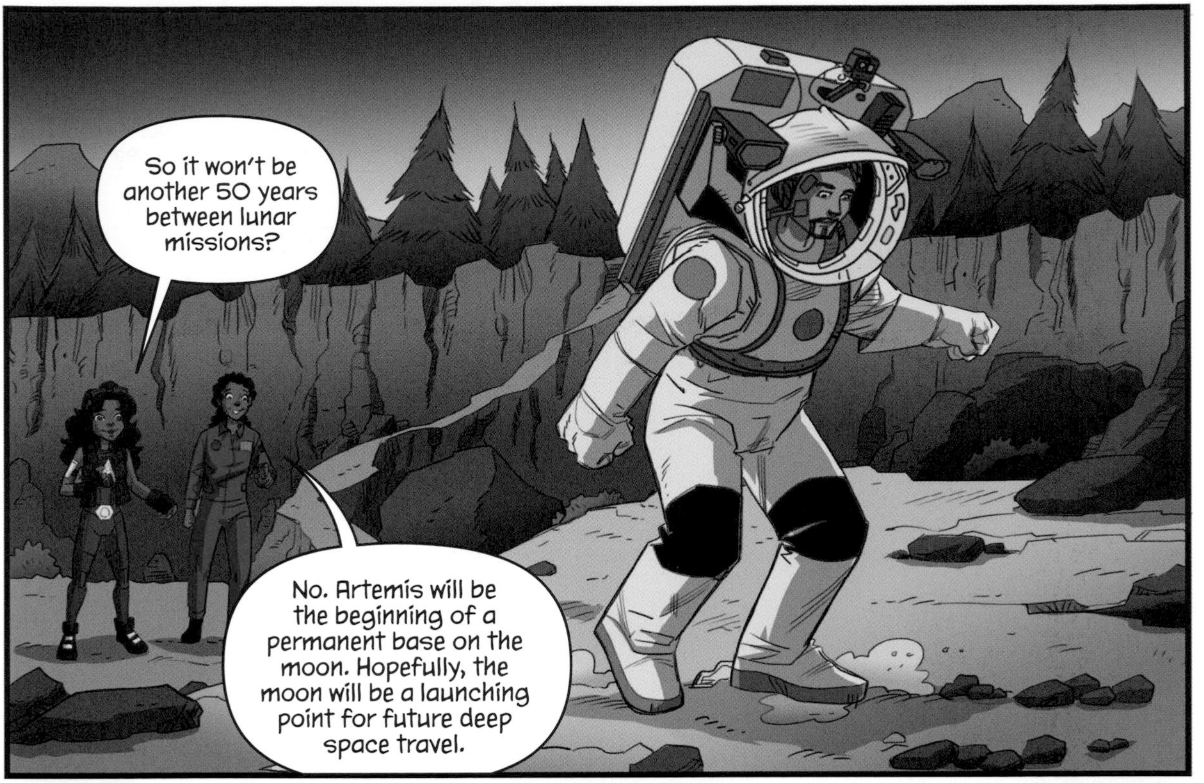
So it won't be another 50 years between lunar missions?
No. Artemis will be the beginning of a permanent base on the moon. Hopefully, the moon will be a launching point for future deep space travel.

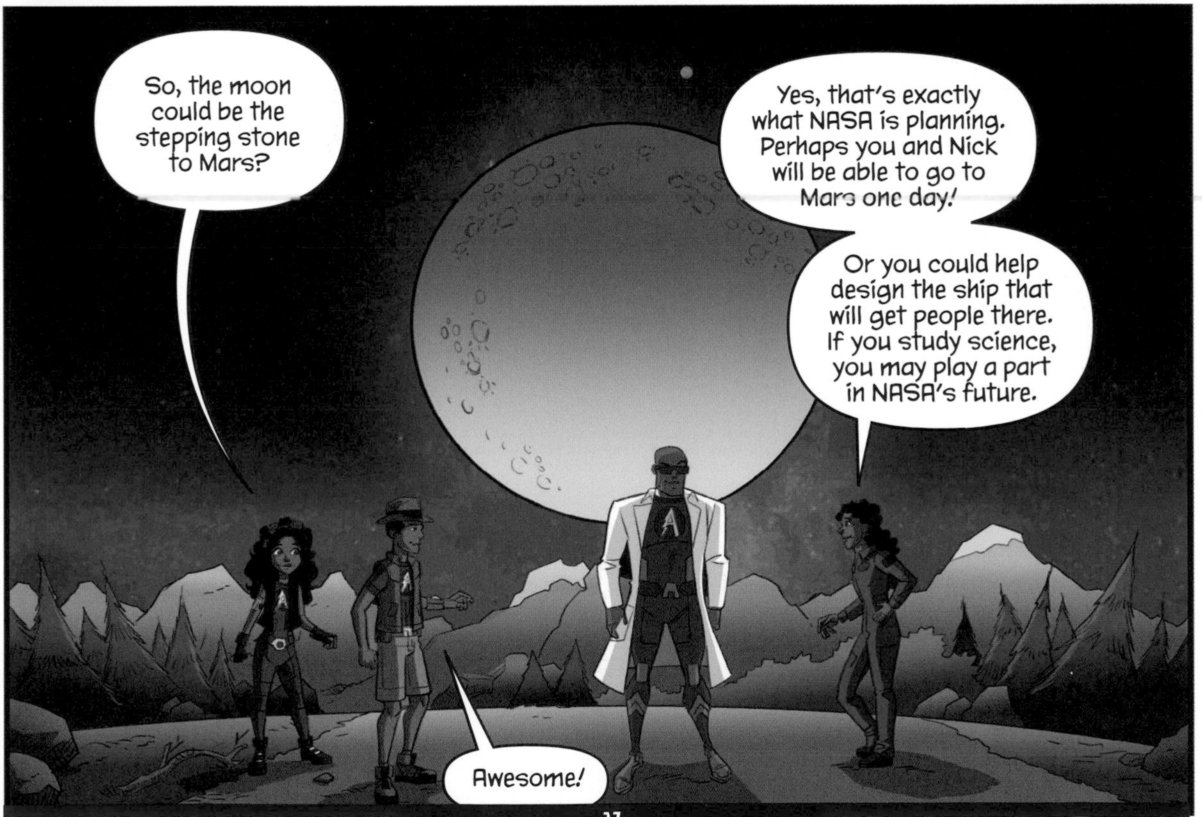
So, the moon could be the stepping stone to Mars?
Yes, that's exactly what NASA is planning. Perhaps you and Nick will be able to go to Mars one day!
Or you could help design the ship that will get people there. If you study science, you may play a part in NASA's future.
Awesome!

MOONWALKING

Since astronauts last walked on the moon, there have been many advances in science and technology. What do we know today, as NASA prepares for the Artemis missions?

- NASA and other nations' space programs have sent several probes and rovers to explore the moon. One probe found evidence that there may be water beneath the moon's surface.

- Lunar orbiters have photographed and mapped the moon's surface in detail. Just as you can see detailed satellite photos of your neighborhood on a computer, we can do the same with the moon. You can even see a complete 3D map of the moon online at: moon3dmap.com.

- NASA has developed several new advanced composite materials. They are used in everything from rockets to spacesuits. These materials are stronger and lighter than the materials used for the Apollo missions.

- Computers are used to control nearly all functions on a spacecraft. Computers today are far faster and more powerful than those used for the Apollo missions. Today's smart phones can store 7 million times more information than the computer on Apollo 11. Even the calculator you use for math problems is 350 times faster than the Apollo computer.

- The Apollo missions were led by the United States. But Artemis will be an international project, with the help of other nations' space programs. NASA recognizes that other nations have advanced technology that can help reach its goals.

- All 12 astronauts who walked on the moon from 1969 to 1972 were white men. Artemis will bring the first women and people of color to the moon.

GLOSSARY

civilian (si-VIL-yuhn)—a person who is not in the military

composite (kuhm-PAH-zuht)—a material made from a mixture of plastic and other chemicals or metals

crater (KRAY-tuhr)—a hole made when a large rock, such as an asteroid or meteorite, crashes into the surface of a planet or moon

electromagnetic waves (i-LEK-troh-mag-NET-ik WAYVZ)—waves of energy, such as visible light, radio waves, or x-rays

friction (FRIK-shuhn)—a force produced when two objects rub against each other; friction slows down objects

lunar (LOO-nur)—having to do with the moon

terrain (tuh-RAYN)—the surface or type of landscape in a particular place

vacuum (VAK-yoom)—a space that is completely empty of matter, including air and other gases

READ MORE

Buckley Jr., James. *Neil Armstrong: First Man on the Moon!* San Diego: Portable Press Kids, 2021.

Collins, Ailynn. *Exploring the Solar System and Beyond: A Max Axiom Super Scientist Adventure.* North Mankato, MN: Capstone, 2023.

Maranville, Amy. *The Apollo 11 Moon Landing: A Day that Changed America.* North Mankato, MN: Capstone, 2022.

INTERNET SITES

3D Moon Map
moon3dmap.com

The Apollo Missions
nasa.gov/mission_pages/apollo/missions/index.html

NASA: Artemis Program
nasa.gov/artemis/videos

INDEX

advanced materials, 28
Apollo 11 mission, 6–9
Apollo program, 6, 9, 11, 12, 17, 18, 20, 25, 28, 29
Artemis program, 9, 10, 17, 25, 27, 28, 29
astronauts, 6, 7, 9, 10, 14, 15, 16, 17, 20, 21, 28, 29
   Aldrin, Buzz, 8, 11, 23
   Armstrong, Neil, 8, 11, 23
   careers of, 23–24
   Collins, Michael, 8, 23
   Glenn, John, 16
   training of, 22–25

distance to the moon, 7

European Space Agency, 20

lunar research, 11, 28

Mars, 17, 21, 27
moonbase, 27
   resources for, 26

NASA, 6, 9, 10–11, 12, 13, 15, 21, 27, 28, 29
   Glenn Research Center, 16
   Johnson Space Center, 12, 22
   Kennedy Space Center, 12
   Stennis Space Center, 12–13

orbiting the moon, 7, 8, 19, 20, 21

rocket testing, 12–14

spacecraft, 11
   computers of, 29
   Gateway, 21
   Human Landing System (HLS), 21
   International Space Station, 10, 17, 22
   Orion, 15, 17, 18–19, 20, 21
   Saturn rocket, 6, 7, 12
   Space Launch System (SLS), 12, 13, 14–15, 18
   testing of, 16–17
spacesuits, 26, 28
   testing of, 22, 25

temperatures on moon, 26

ABOUT THE AUTHOR

Bruce Berglund was a history professor for 19 years. He taught courses on ancient and modern history, war and society, women's history, and sports history. Bruce was a Fulbright Scholar three times. He has written several books on the history of Eastern Europe in the 20th century and the history of world hockey.